HO PRIMER

model railroading for all

by Linn Westcott

KALMBACH K BOOKS

FIRST EDITION, 1962. SECOND EDITION, 1964. Second printing, 1966. Third printing, 1968. Fourth printing, 1969. Fifth printing, 1971. Sixth printing, 1973. Seventh printing, 1974. Eighth printing, 1975. Ninth printing, 1976. Tenth printing, 1978. Eleventh printing, 1982.

HO = AITCH-O

HO is usually pronounced like letters: "Aitch-O." The letters stand for half-O, meaning half as big as O scale. Actually HO scale is a little bigger than half.

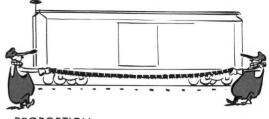

TRACK GAUGE

HO *gauge* refers only to track, not to the models. The standard gauge of real railroads is 4'-8½" measured between the railheads. In HO scale the standard gauge measures .650" (slightly more than ⅝").

PROPORTION

HO scale models are made 1/87 as big as the real thing. You could couple 87 HO boxcars end to end and they'd stretch as long as one real boxcar.

WORKING IN SCALE

A 4-foot sidewalk along an HO scale street would be four times 9/64" wide, or 9/16". In this simple way you can figure anything in HO size. (But we recommend that you get an HO scale rule.)

Basic HO information

SCALE FOOT

The sizes of HO models are usually measured in scale feet, which are, of course, 1/87 as big as real feet. An HO scale foot is 9/64".* This is no problem, for you can buy a "scale rule" marked in HO scale feet.

*The official scale for HO is actually 3.5 mm. per foot, and this is the standard used in making scale rules. However, lacking a scale rule you can use the 9/64"-per-foot figure with an error of only 2 per cent. This is not serious except on the most exact models. A more accurate makeshift scheme is to use an architect's ⅛" scale and add 10 per cent to all measurements. The error is then trivial.

12 VOLTS D.C. FOR TOP SPEED

While HO trains often run fast enough on lower voltages, 12 v. d.c. is the maximum needed for engines. Most power packs furnish this at full load.

COUPLER POSITION

Most HO cars and locomotives come with couplers of the horn-hook type (often miscalled "NMRA couplers"). Advanced workers often substitute other types of couplers. In any case, the centers of couplers should be adjusted to ride 25/64" above railtops and uncoupling pins should clear switchwork rails by a full 1/32".

PARALLEL TRACK

You may be told that 2" spread, center to center, is enough for double tracks and in yards, but this is not enough when the tracks curve at sharper than 36" radius. Trains may sideswipe.

HILLS AND VALLEYS

Grades of 2" rise in 100" (called 2 per cent) are easy; for short trains 4 per cent grades are adequate. A track must rise at least 3½" to pass above another track.

THEY CALLED IT "HALF-O"

HO was first used in England (but a larger scale called OO, 4 mm. to the foot, is more commonly used on the same track in England today). HO has been sold in the U.S. since 1934, but it wasn't until the forties that it became the most popular scale for adult model railroading. HO trains for young folks came in the mid-fifties, but with more emphasis on the creative features than on the train as a toy.

GIL REID

22" CURVES

The track in train sets and on small table railroads is usually made to 18" radius, but curves of 24" or in a pinch 22" radius are preferable if you want to operate larger locomotives, passenger cars, or long trains. Radius is measured to the centerline between rails.

1: How to get more fun out of HO trains

SOMETIMES trains are thought of as toys, but the reason so many men have found HO railroading intriguing is because HO doesn't have to be a toy in any sense of the word. HO offers so much for you to do, to think about, to enjoy, that it is one of the most creative and rewarding hobbies you could possibly have.

Of course, HO railroading is for fun, so how you go about it is for you to decide. Some of us already in the hobby will tell you that this way or that is the only way to do something. Follow our advice if you wish, but if you want to do something your own way, go ahead. Just remember to have fun.

Some of Bill McClanahan's work is shown in this book on page 4. I wish you could see it in actuality. Many experts in our HO hobby get their satisfaction from building the most detailed models you can imagine. If you like precise, skillful work, join them and work your way to the top. But don't get the idea that that's the only way to have fun in HO. You can have fun with some sorry-looking cars and engines too. You can simulate the operations of a railroad yard in detail; your equipment need not be perfect but it must run well. You'll have to pick a balance between skill and operating fun for yourself, because you may not have the time to create both perfectly detailed models and perfectly worked-out train operations.

The same goes for the cost of HO equipment. You can get a big railroad operating soon and have it always free of mechanical trouble if you have the money to do so. But money is only a timesaver in HO. You can build all the HO railroad you want at a very small expense if you can put lots of time into it. Again, you'll have to strike your own balance, setting your sights for the sensible level of your own time and income.

If you're a teenager, you'll want to concentrate on the more complicated kits, on scenery, on painting equipment, on anything that provides you with many hours of fun for the dollar spent. If you're a doctor or dentist with a heavy schedule, you'll most likely want quite a bit of ready-made equipment so you can get the railroad going with less of your personal time.

Of course, even a teenager with time to build complicated kits is better off if he tries kits which gradually increase in difficulty. I've listed many makes of kits in approximate order of complication and time required in the kit-building section, chapter 14.

Unexpected fun

I'd like to make one suggestion about HO that may bring you fun in places you don't expect to find it. Occasionally try something you aren't so sure you will like. For instance, a lot of model railroaders avoid building scenery. I'm sure at least half of these men would like it if they once got the screen tacked down and the first layer of plaster poured on. Scenery isn't discussed in this book because we wanted to do a more complete job on the get-started subjects. But I highly recommend that you find out about scenery, and any other phase of the hobby that doesn't look too attractive at first. Then try to build a little now, and try it again in a year or two when things will look much different to you.

There's another unexpected place where you can have fun in HO, and I'll be repeating this idea from time to time throughout this book. Nothing in HO has to be permanent. You can change your railroad over and over again. Change the whole thing, or change a corner or a station lot. There is a tendency for us to think that everything we put down is final, but we haven't the space to do it that way really. You may have boundless energy for a hobby and you may have lots of ideas too. You cannot execute them all at once, so why not one after another? Keep a photographic record of each new development on your railroad so you can look back at the photos later on when things are all changed around.

Cars and locomotives can change, too. I've tried several color schemes on my engines and passenger cars in the last few months, and I've repainted some freight cars and used decals to letter them because I didn't care for the original color or texture of the paint job. Some plastic cars, for instance, have a waxy look and I quickly repaint them. On locomotives, I add parts (which can be purchased separately) to get a different version of a locomotive.

Finally, there will be times when you may be so tired you don't know what you want to do. This is the adult equivalent of a youngster saying, "Daddy, what can I do now?" Nothing seems to satisfy. Well, in HO, some phase of the hobby will be just right for you when you're in this mood. For me, weathering cars as explained on page 50 is such a lift. Sometimes putting together an otherwise too simple kit has the same relaxing result. Find out what part of HO is a lift for you and use it. It will overcome boredom.

One of the country's best-known modelers, Bill McClan-ahan, has collected some material from other builders to increase the yard facilities in the town of Bruzdenbleedn on Bill's Texas & Rio Grande Western RR. The coaling tower in the background was built from old tin cans by Earl Cochrane. John Allen drew the plans for the en-ginehouse in the foreground. The crack streamliner eases into the station while a freight waits alongside.

Along the right of way

G. Martin Allen decided to go a bit further than the manufacturer did and added more detail to these two kit locomotives. The Roundhouse Prairie, left, has been decked out with an assortment of new parts made by Kemtron and Warren. The Mantua switcher has been sub-jected to even more extensive changes. Martin also used Kemtron and Warren parts on it, in addition to building a new cab and converting the tender from coal to oil fuel.

Although the trackwork in this scene on B. J. Oram's Beaver Valley RR. might look complicated, it really is not. All necessary components to build a bustling industrial center like this can be purchased already assembled. Busy areas with lots of opportunity for a man interested in switching are common on the BV. Surprisingly, this pike is built in a space only 8 feet square.

Some folks prefer to have their model railroads built for them, like the Russell Janick family of Milwaukee, who asked John Lahmayer to build this layout. John used commercial structures, trees, cars, engines and track products in building the raliroad, which is an L-shaped design on two sheets of plywood. Below: The same pike.

John Sawyer's railroad features scenery — lots of it! The White Mountains of New Hampshire dominate this scene on the White River Junction Division of the Boston & Maine and Central Vermont railroads. Here the B&M and the Central parallel each other across the White River. John's mountains are actual rocks inserted into plaster and then painted with tempera watercolors.

2: Starting with a train set

AN HO train set furnishes you with everything you need to get a train going except a power pack. Because of this convenience and because equipment sold in sets saves a little over the cost of parts bought separately, many model railroaders get started in HO with a train set.

Hobby shops generally stock the greatest variety in train sets a month before Christmas, but some have them all year around. In a typical season, there are some 100 different sets of trains ranging from a locomotive and three cars to those containing two locomotives, 10 cars and a pair of switches. Train sets are made by about a dozen different factories, but unlike the old toy railroads, nearly all makes are made to work together on the same track with the same couplers and the same electric current — a tremendous advantage.

Quality versus price

The most popular train sets are medium priced. They have enough cars to be a lot of fun to run, and if you buy only a little extra track, you can do switching.

Higher priced sets offer you either more cars and locomotives, or else about the same number of cars and pieces of track but with a high-quality locomotive. Naturally a locomotive with quality gears instead of a rubber-band drive, with a metal instead of plastic body shell, with more wheels, or with a better motor, will cost more even though it looks the same in outward details. Some of the best engines cannot be found in any train set. They are only sold separately.

Fig. 2-1. You can start an HO railroad on a rug and plan its design before building or buying a train table, but the rug is not satisfactory very long.

I don't mean to scoff at rubberband drives or plastic bodies; they give good service, adequate for most of us. But you'll also prize the supreme performance of a well-made geared locomotive and the added pulling power you get with a metal body due to the extra weight. The slower geared locomotives also can pull more cars without overheating their motors.

The smallest HO sets are low on the amount of track and the number of cars provided. You cannot do much switching or railroadlike train operation with only three cars, so the smallest sets are just a way to get started at low cost.

This doesn't mean that small sets are of low quality. Except for novelty sets that are easy to recognize as toys, small HO train sets have the same quality cars and locomotives as the medium-sized sets. The difference is in the amount of equipment you get and in the simplicity of the locomotive. Often small sets come with four-wheel switching locomotives of one sort or another, types never actually seen pulling trains on a main line. However, if you start this way, the small loco will take its place nicely as a switcher when your railroad has grown larger and when you have added a mainline locomotive or two.

Fig. 2-2. Mantua, also known as Tyco, makes one of the smallest HO train sets as well as larger sets. Locomotive shown is a steam-type "tank switcher" with four driving wheels. On real railroads such small switchers are not used for mainline trains but on model railroads switchers are often used to get the railroad started. Larger steam types come in certain train sets. Mantua's cars have metal frames for weight, and plastic bodies.

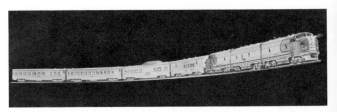

Fig. 2-3. Larger train sets with diesel locomotives will usually include two or three engine units, but only the first will actually have a motor. You can buy extra motored units, of course, but the extra power isn't needed for any but very, very long model trains. This is a set by Athearn, with streamlined passenger cars. Both steam and diesel, passenger and freight, are available in sets and in many styles of equipment. However, model railroaders actually buy much more freight equipment than passenger. Both freight and passenger cars can be bought separately.

Fig. 2-4. Some HO models like this set from AHM are made in Europe. Car wheels made in Europe have different standards from those made in the United States, but since replacing wheels (if necessary) is not costly, we can use the imported European materials satisfactorily. As is true with American-made equipment, the foreign-made trains operate on 12 volts direct current, and the cars and locomotives are equipped with horn-hook couplers.

Fig. 2-5. In HO you can get oldtime American trains like Mantua's Civil War trains, and modern British or European trains—and here's an oldtime German train, made by Fleischmann, that looks as if it came from a storybook.

Track in train sets

Train sets include a circle of track—usually 12 pieces to a circle — and a few straight sections to spread the circle into an oval or rounded square. The two-train sets may include two switches so you can put one train on the side track while the other goes by it. In no instance does a train set have enough track for you to do more than the most rudimentary switching and train operation. Most model railroaders get a few more switches and other pieces of track very soon. There are several books with good track plans you can follow.* You can pick a plan to fit the track you have and then add to it later.

Usually the track in a train set is

*Simple track plans divided into sections can be found in the book *Track Plans for Sectional Track.* Those in the rear of that book will be the most fun to operate. Track manufacturers also give away and sell track plan booklets to promote their own lines. Actually most makes of HO track are compatible.

While not divided into track sections for you (not really necessary), the plans in the book *101 Track Plans* offer a wide range of small to large layouts compactly designed which you can copy literally, or, better still, use as a basis for making variations. The text in *101 Track Plans* is often overlooked but is extremely worthwhile reading.

In choosing a plan, prefer one that allows you to do lots of wayside switching as well as mainline running. Wayside spurs can usually be added to a plan even if not originally shown.

18" radius, which means a circle 36" across plus the width of the track, total about 37¼" of table space. All train-set locomotives and cars will run on this track, but larger custom and kit HO locomotives require track of 22", or even greater, radius.

Some train sets have track of 15" radius to fit a table only 31¼" square, or 16" for a 33¼" table. Occasionally even sharper track is used, but all of this very sharp track should be used only when you haven't space for larger curves. If you get larger curves, save the tight ones for industrial sidings or a streetcar line or the like. In any case, since additional track is inexpensive, it should have little to do with your choice of a train set.

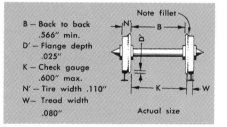

B — Back to back .566" min.
D' — Flange depth .025"
K — Check gauge .600" max.
N' — Tire width .110"
W — Tread width .080"

Note fillet
Actual size

Fig. 2-6. NMRA RP25 wheels for HO.

Importance of good wheels

Competition is an important factor in the train-set market and thus price is a big consideration. For this reason the trucks (sets of four or six wheels at the ends of each car) are not always of ideal quality. On the other hand, in the serious hobby of HO railroading, quality performance is more important than cheapest price. Fortunately you can get excellent trucks at a reasonable price, and many model railroaders make a practice of replacing any trucks they happen to get that are of only fair quality.

Wheels can give poor performance if their treads and flanges are not of the best shape. Sharp-edged or deep flanges cause derailments by snagging on rail joints and in track switches. Deep flanges also lift wheels off the track in crossings and switches.

Some makers use the RP25 wheel shape shown in Fig. 2-6. It gives excellent performance.

Trucks that will not roll their car down a grade of 1" in 3 feet might also be considered for replacement, as easy roll also reduces derailments and allows you to pull longer trains as well.

3: A power pack is essential

THE correct electric supply for running HO trains is 12 volts direct current (12 v. d.c.).* Most model railroaders buy a "power pack" for running trains. The power pack looks like a toy train transformer but contains more parts. It contains an electronic "switch" that changes the alternating current that all transformers

*Most European trains use this same 12 v. d.c. standard, but Maerklin trains are not compatible with American HO and require special power and special track. Trix trains are special, but convertible.

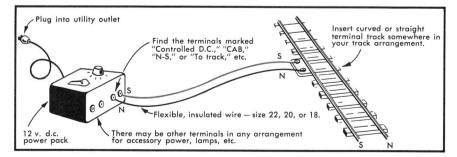

Plug into utility outlet

Find the terminals marked "Controlled D.C.," "CAB," "N-S," or "To track," etc.

Insert curved or straight terminal track somewhere in your track arrangement.

Flexible, insulated wire — size 22, 20, or 18.

12 v. d.c. power pack

There may be other terminals in any arrangement for accessory power, lamps, etc.

Fig. 3-1. Basic power pack connections for running one HO scale model train.

Don't use a transformer for HO!

Fig. 3-2. Because HO locomotive motors run only on d.c., they stall and get warm if you try to run them on a.c., and might burn out. However, you can use a.c. from a toy train transformer if you add a conversion rectifier (Lionel's shown with American Flyer transformer, but any conversion rectifier can be used with any toy train transformer). The combination is equal to a power pack.

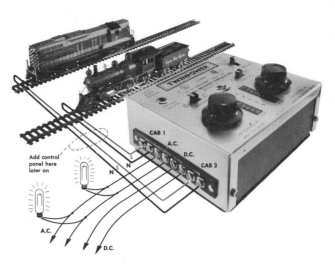

Fig. 3-3. Power packs with built-in rectifier and transformer come in many sizes. This one, manufactured by the Model Rectifier Corp., has an extra throttle to handle a second train. Other connections are usually available for accessories. This pack has "Cab" connections for two separate trains. The a.c. terminals are for lamps and other accessories; the d.c. terminals are handy for switch machines or accessories that require d.c. power.

produce into the direct current we need. The electronic switch is actually a pair or quad of "rectifiers."

Very few train sets are sold with power packs and you can buy power packs in many sizes and with interesting features, so in buying a pack, consider these things:

Over-all quality.
Power rating.
Control features and extras.
Accessory connections.

We'll discuss these features in that order and then show how to connect the power pack to the track.

Quality

Most model railroad power packs are adequate electrically. They can deliver power to one or more trains depending on rating, and deliver full rated power at a full 12 volts. But there are mechanical differences that affect quality.

A de luxe quality pack will be able to slow the lightest, easiest-running locomotive down to a crawl and a smooth stop. Ordinary quality power packs may not be able to do this, while poor packs may produce a sudden jump between some speeds or stopping. Poor packs often have handles that get floppy or come off completely.

Toggle, lever, and knob-type switches cost the manufacturer more, so they are found mostly on the better packs. Let me repeat, however, that the trains will run about the same, except for low speeds and smoothness of control, with any quality of power pack. If you intend to let a train run

around and around, hardly ever changing speed, a quality pack could be an extravagance.

Power rating

Sometimes a power pack is rated as able to run "two trains," or maybe several. This is misleading. Unless a pack has extra speed-control throttle handles for the extra trains, it isn't convenient for running more than one train. Such large one-throttle packs are really "two-locomotive" packs with extra capacity so two engines can be used on the same train.

The accurate way to rate a power pack is in the amperes it can deliver continuously at 12 v. without overheating. Roughly, each locomotive with its headlight takes 1 ampere of current; thus a "3 a. power pack" can run three locomotives at once. Each group of 6 flashlight size or 10

grain-of-wheat size lights in cars also takes about an ampere of current. If you have a locomotive with a smoke unit, add an extra ½a. Add all the amperes and make sure the pack is rated high enough.

If you run lights in your scenery from the same power pack, count another ampere for each 6 or 10 of them.

Packs to run two or more trains

When you run more than one train, you should have separate speed-control levers for each train. These can be included on the same power pack or else separately on more than one power pack. Here are three schemes:

THROTTLE UNITS. These are boxes containing a throttle and reversing switch which you can add to nearly any make of power pack to get separate control for another train.

You can use any throttle unit with any make of power pack providing the pack has terminals for the connection. See B in Fig. 3-4. Throttle units keep the initial cost of power down since you don't buy a unit until you need it. Another advantage is that the second throttle can be used at some distance from the pack. This is more convenient for father-and-son or two-man operation. You can even carry a small throttle unit at the end of a cable and walk around while you run and switch a train.

TWO- and THREE-THROTTLE PACKS. Some power packs come with two or three speed-control handles built in. Their advantage is only a matter of cost and of compactness. More often

No dangerous electricity

The electric current that runs HO trains is low-voltage electricity, a pressure so low you cannot get a serious shock. It is also reasonably safe from the danger of fire. You could leave a power pack turned on all the time and little electricity would be wasted. But if anything should ever go wrong, it could cause overheating. So it is a good idea to leave the power off if you are not using the railroad.

than not it would be better to buy two separate power packs.

These multithrottle packs come in two varieties. Some have internal connections between the throttles and some do not. Unfortunately, few dealers know which is which, nor do they realize why this is important.* The packs with internal connections (and also the combination of a pack plus a side throttle as just described) both share the fault of being incompatible with Atlas block control components or with any "common-rail" type of wiring scheme. This is too involved to explain here (see the book *How to Wire Your Model Railroad*, chapter 3), but both the side-throttle scheme and the two- or three-throttle pack (if it has internal connections) make for more complicated track wiring if one plans to expand to a railroad running two or more trains on the same trackage.

There is one exception. The type of control panel described later in this book supplies the necessary special wiring rather painlessly.

MULTIPLE POWER SUPPLY. This long name refers to the idea of using a separate power pack for each additional train, and you gain several advantages by doing this. You can use any of a great variety of packs, and even if you choose low-cost packs you'll get good performance when they handle only one train each (Fig. 3-4, D). This scheme does not have the wiring disadvantages mentioned before.

Model railroaders who like the electrical side of HO railroading also prefer this multiple-pack idea because it allows the wiring of signals, common rail, cab control, and other advanced control schemes to be simpler. I'd call it the best method except where total cost or the convenience of having more throttles in one box is important.

Control features

You need a throttle lever or knob and a reversing switch for each train you will run at one time. In addition, each power pack should have an on-off switch. In a good pack these controls will be easy to use, and will have a good feel when operated. The pack should have provision for mounting below the edge of a table in preference to setting it on top (where it's often in the way).

Every power pack is safer with some sort of protection against short circuits. The simplest is a fuse that slips into clips. But if your pack has this, buy a little thermal circuit breaker that slips into the same clips. In the

*Connect a voltmeter between either output terminal of throttle 1 and one output terminal of throttle 2. Turn the throttles on and throw the two reversing switches to all possible positions. If the voltmeter gives a reading in any switch position, there are unwanted internal connections in the power pack.

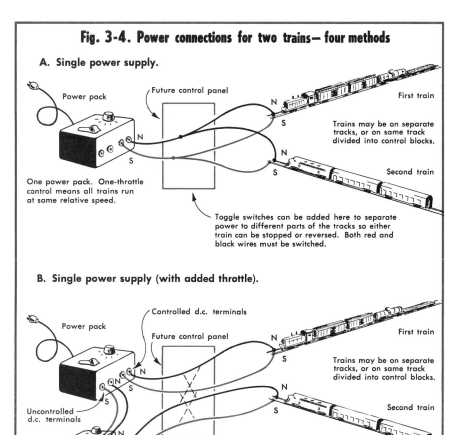

Fig. 3-4. Power connections for two trains— four methods

A. Single power supply.

Power pack

Future control panel

N
S
First train

Trains may be on separate tracks, or on same track divided into control blocks.

N
S
Second train

One power pack. One-throttle control means all trains run at same relative speed.

Toggle switches can be added here to separate power to different parts of the tracks so either train can be stopped or reversed. Both red and black wires must be switched.

B. Single power supply (with added throttle).

Power pack

Controlled d.c. terminals

Future control panel

N
S
First train

Trains may be on separate tracks, or on same track divided into control blocks.

N
S
Second train

Uncontrolled d.c. terminals

Added throttle unit

Second throttle allows each train to run at an independent speed.

Toggle switches may be added here so either throttle can control any part of track. Both red and black wires must be switched.

C. Single power supply (with multithrottle power pack).

Power pack

Future control panel

N
S
First train

Trains may be on separate tracks, or on same track divided into control blocks.

N
S
Second train

Although second throttle is built in, the result is the same as drawing B; trains have separate speed control. Pack could have three or more throttles.

Toggle switches may be added here so either throttle can control any part of track. Both red and black wires must be switched unless you are sure pack is free of internal connections. See text.

D. Multiple power supply.

First power pack

Common power return from all N rail connections. This is called "common-rail."

Future control panel

N
S
First train

Trains may be on separate tracks, or on same track divided into control blocks.

N
S
Second train

Second power pack

Second power pack allows separate speed control of second train.

Toggle switches may be added here so either power pack can control any part of track. Only red wires must be switched, which makes wiring simpler.

The control panel in this book works equally well with all four arrangements.

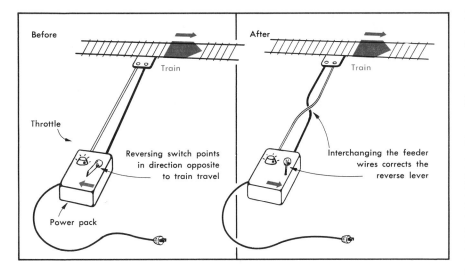

Fig. 3-5. Change wires so trains go in same direction as reversing lever.

long run it's cheaper. Test it to see if the breaker "pops" open if you short-circuit the output terminals for about 10 seconds. After it cools off, push the spring back in place gently. You can bend the spring gently to adjust its action. Many packs have good built-in circuit breakers.

Besides these features on a power pack, there are optional features that you can take or leave. A long throttle handle has a prototype look. Some packs have circuit breakers that work like the modern toggle breakers in newer houses. Some packs have lamps to show when power is on or when you have a short circuit. Some even have voltmeters and ammeters so you can see how your locomotives perform; with these, hunting for electrical troubles is also easier.

The control circuit

You don't have to know anything about electricity to run HO trains, but a little knowledge about it can save you from having to call for help from another model railroader every time something goes awry.

Fig. 3-6 shows the basic circuit that makes trains run. The important thing here is the pattern. Notice how electricity can flow only when there's a complete loop for it to go around. The power pack acts like a pump and it pushes electrons out of its minus, or negative, terminal. If there is an all-metal path from here to the positive terminal, the electricity can move; when it does it creates heat in the wire and magnetism around it.

When the metal path isn't complete, the electricity stops flowing even though the pack is still trying to push it. It's like water pressure behind a closed valve. Electric pressure is measured in volts.

Dirt on the rails can lift the wheels and break the all-metal loop or "circuit." Then electricity stops and so does the motor. The pressure is there but it can't push through the dirt because the pressure is only 12 v. on a model railroad. A much higher voltage could actually

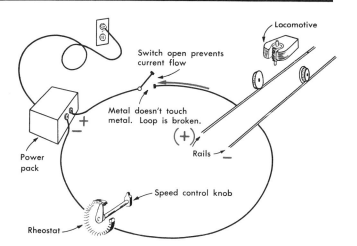

Fig. 3-7. Rheostat or open switch restricts the current.

push current right through the dirt, but that would be too much pressure for the trains.

A broken wire or poor screw connection can also break the all-metal path. Loose rail joiners are the worst offenders.

Sometimes we want to stop the train; then we deliberately break the all-metal path with an electric switch. The terms for a switch are just the opposite to those for a water valve. We say an electric switch is open when it turns the current off to stop the train. We say the switch is closed when it lets the current flow.

If you wanted to run a train slowly, you could open and close the switch rapidly to let the motor get power only part of the time, but this isn't practical. Another way, and one often used, is to install a "rheostat" in the circuit. This is like a switch except that it gradually restricts the flow of current.

It accomplishes this by wasting some of the pressure so the rest of the loop gets less. In this way the motor isn't pushed so hard. To run a good locomotive at medium speed, you need only 6 v. of pressure, so the other 6 v. is wasted in the rheostat.

Both the on-off switch and the rheostat are usually contained inside the power pack. But you could connect them at any place around the loop since the same electricity makes the entire circuit. See Fig. 3-7.

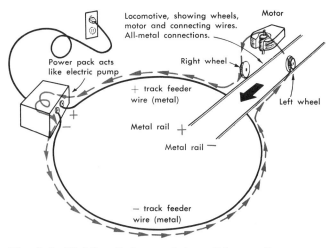

Fig. 3-6. Metal path is complete and locomotive moves.

One-train wiring

The better transistor-throttle power packs cost much more than other packs, but they give the best control of all. They usually have extra knobs to adjust the action to match the needs of each individual train and thus can start and run the train very smoothly.

Accessory connections available

The two main terminals on the power pack are for connecting the wires to the track. Most packs have additional terminals, and usually two of these provide alternating current (a.c.) at about 16 v. You can connect lamps and remote-control switches to these terminals as long as you haven't used up all the ampere-rating in running the train. Some packs have additional terminals for "uncontrolled" d.c. as mentioned under Fig. 3-3.

Occasionally packs have additional a.c. terminals at lower voltages either for special accessories or for lamps. In any case, if the electrical terminals are not clearly marked on the pack or its instruction sheet, have your hobby shop dealer check them with his meters and mark them for you. A good way is to use dabs of colored dope like this:

Red-black: d.c. to the track.

Orange-green: plus and minus uncontrolled d.c. Orange is plus; green is minus.

Yellow-yellow: a.c. for accessories.

Since there's a reversing switch in the controlled d.c. to the track, there's no such thing as a permanent plus or minus terminal here and two black marks or no marking at all would also be sufficient.

Pulse power

A peculiarity of small motors is that they tend to jump from a standstill rather than start smoothly, due to unevenness of the magnet's pull in the motor. This jerking is at its worst when running with pure direct current from a battery or filter. The current from an ordinary power pack is better because it contains ripples of strength that overcome the magnetic locking before the average voltage (which determines running speed) is so high. Some power packs have a switch which decreases the average voltage for a given throttle setting (by supplying half-wave power rather than full-wave) and thus operate balky motors even more smoothly at slow speeds. For pulling full-length trains, regular power (which actually has some mild pulse anyway) should be switched on, as the full-strength pulse power produces more heat for given work in the motor. Too much pulse can also polish the wheels and reduce traction.

Some transistor throttles can provide continuously adjustable pulse power for ideal motor matching.

Connecting simple track patterns

Our HO sectional track is so designed that there is no problem of any kind in connecting a simple track pattern for one-train operation. You need one terminal section of track, which can be obtained in either a straight or curved piece. If it has the proper radius, a curved piece is handier since much more of a small railroad is on curves than straight. (See Fig. 3-1).

Just connect the two wires from the "controlled d.c." terminals of the power pack to the two terminals of the track. The electricity will then run through all the pieces of track you add on — straight, curved, or switches. Wherever your train goes, the current will reach it.

It doesn't really matter which wire of the terminal track connects to which of the two power-pack connections as long as they both go to the controlled d.c. terminals. However, you may find it more convenient to try the wires both ways around (see Fig. 3-5) and arrange them whichever way results in having the reversing lever on the power pack point in the direction the train will go.

For such short lengths of wire, the size you use isn't very important. Sizes as small as No. 24 will run trains perfectly, but No. 20 is often used. No. 18 is used on larger railroads, but is a little stiff for small table and rug railroads. Stranded wire is more flexible than solid, so it is usually perferred. It has one fault — small strands can easily bend away and touch a nearby terminal on the power pack or track and cause an unnoticed short circuit.

The two wires are all you need for one-train operation unless your track plan happens to include a "return loop" or a "wye." You might not suspect you have these, but if either or both of these features are hidden in your track plan, you'll find the train won't run and the circuit breaker snaps open on the power pack, perhaps after a few seconds of heating up. Often this first occurs after you have added a track switch to connect one part of the line over to another place. The special wiring needed for loops and wyes is shown on page 27.

4: Good train performance

SOME time ago a fellow visited the offices of MODEL RAILROADER magazine and looked at some railroad projects we happened to be building at the time. He enjoyed watching a train running on a test oval and then commented:

"I tried HO a couple of years ago, but I went back to my three-rail trains. HO trains were too slow for me."

If our visitor could have seen a finished railroad I'd have shown him how much faster trains seem to go when run through a completed scene with fences, trees, telephone poles, buildings and bridges. It's very true that HO trains just seem to be crawling along when they may really

Fig. 4-1. Contact cleaning fluid restores operation immediately on oxidized wheels or rails. Wipe, brush or spray it onto a short section of rails only. Wheels will spread it farther.

How to clean rails

be going 60 scale miles per hour. That's a foot a second. But HO trains are only ⅛₇ as big as real trains and if you put real trains on a giant-sized flat table and backed away 87 times the normal viewing distance, real trains would look mighty slow too.

You can speed up HO trains to faster than normal speed with little harm to them other than faster wear. But my point is that the more satisfying way to get speed in the long run is to work toward the creation of a realistic scene with lots of detail. Then get your eyes close to the track for some of the most thrilling and speedy railroad scenes you ever saw. Even when trains are viewed from a distance, poles, fences, etc., create the effect of speed.

Two things that can spoil the illusion of correct speed are sudden starts and sudden stops. A transistorized power pack or a skilled operator with any good power pack can start the train gradually, and then correct speeds look correct.

Regardless of speed, what we want most in HO railroad operation is dependable performance. After that we want smooth control of speed, coupling, uncoupling, stops and starts. All are very possible and if you don't get satisfaction some very simple thing may be the cause.

Dirty track is common

Dirty track is the most common cause of trouble. It and dirty wheels are often the real cause of sluggish operation when you might suspect broken wires, weak motors, or a defective power pack. You can buy rail cleaning fluids, although I find few hobby shops have them in stock. Such fluids remove gummy dirt — a long-time accumulation of drying oils and dust — which gives a great deal of trouble on steel rail. Only once in a great while do you have to clean such dark dirt from brass rail.

Brass rail and brass wheels work very well until the minute film of oil on their surfaces wears off. Then if you let the trains lay idle for a day or two, a layer of oxide forms that you don't see, and which doesn't conduct electricity. This acts like a thin layer of baked enamel. You can remove the oxide chemically or by wearing it off. The usual symptom of oxide is hesitating, sluggish operation and sparking at the wheels.

Many model railroaders scrub the oxide off with rubber erasers that contain a little abrasive. This restores train operation, but unfortunately the scratches left behind tend to collect dirt and then increase the rate of oxidation.

I have had excellent results with an all-liquid treatment which is applied to the track only every few weeks. I first found the fluid, No-Ox, at

radio supply stores that carry the Walsco line of supplies. Contactene is almost as good. These are contact protecting fluids intended for electric switches, pushbuttons, relay blades and the like, as well as for volume controls. They cut dirt and oxidation on HO track as well as on wheels.

The treatment is most simple. Apply the fluid to the top of each rail, in 2" or 3" stretches spaced 30 feet apart, or at places where trouble is evident. Then run a locomotive with a number of cars ahead of it over the various lines. The car wheels will distribute the fluid between the places where you applied it and thus the rails will not be so wet as to affect traction.

On the first trip, operation should be much improved. If wheels and rail are dirty, this dirt will be loosened and you can wipe it from the rails with a rag. The wheels will carry more dirt from inaccessible track (as in tunnels) to where you can wipe it off.

These fluids are available in spray cans for handy application in places you could not otherwise reach. Careful — too much spray softens plastic.

The new nickel silver rail seems to be fairly free of trouble from oxide, but brass wheels may still need an occasional treatment. Even when rail is clean, any locomotive that hasn't been operated for a few days may have to be run through a trace of the fluid to cut oxide on its wheels.

5: Fun with little railroads—and big

MOST of my experiences have been with rather large model railroads, but in 1957 and 1958 I had in my home the railroad described in the book *The HO Railroad That Grows.* This was designed to get the most out of a 4 x 8-foot plywood table. Inwardly I sort of scoffed at the idea of such a railroad having much in the line of possibilities for continued fun. So did my son Paul, then 14 years old. We had the small railroad only for a short while before we began to realize how much it could challenge us. While we have started another larger railroad since, this little one gave us far more satisfaction than we expected.

The enlightenment came at the time when we had all the bugs out of the track and had located and fixed a mis-

take in one of the track feeder wires. (Table railroads don't always work perfectly the first time.) In a way, the completion of the road to the point where it worked perfectly seemed to leave nothing more to do. We were in limbo, happy or at least contented, but with nothing to do.

Things didn't stay that way for long. With things working well, Paul began to experiment. He tried two locomotives on the same train and learned that some engines will work together while others won't. He began to run two trains at the same time and immediately discovered it takes a little skill to do it well, not just flipping power on and off but starting and slowing each train gradually, like real trains. Our control panel was similar

to the simple one in this book, which allows separate control of each train everywhere.

Next we began to do a little switching. We installed uncoupling ramps and found the couplers on some cars had to be adjusted a little more carefully for uncoupling than for coupling. We began to make up trains in the yard and send them out on the main line, around several times and then over an upper-level line that turned them to go the other way. Then a few laps more in the other direction and the train was back in the yard.

This introduced another problem. The train entered the yard head first, so we had to let the locomotive escape to another track before it was of any use to us for another train. Likewise we had to figure a place to put the caboose until another train was made.

Up to this time my younger son, Russell, then 10, was only a little interested in the railroad. He spent more time shooting down cowboys in front of the miniature stores. But now he became intrigued with running a second train. He didn't like switching it in the yard very much, but he did like to run it around many times trying to meet the first train here and then there as it went.

Well, if the boys in your family are like Paul and Russell, you can imagine some of the arguments that might come up. For instance, Paul's train started out of a sidetrack headed for a sort of horseshoe curve we had running around a lake. At the same time, Russell's train headed for the same curve from the other direction. The trains couldn't hit because the electrical polarity is changed at a section

break; but just the same there was a problem: Which train should back up?

Well, we borrowed a book of train rules and studied them to see what a real railroad would do about it.

We found the rules that prototype railroads use cover many things that didn't concern us, but we did adopt these simple rules:

1. Passenger trains have the right of way over freight trains going in either direction.
2. Otherwise, the train going "eastbound" (counterclockwise) has the right of way over the other train.
3. Switching trains using the main line have no rights at all.

This worked to a point, but it worked perfectly after we introduced a new rule not borrowed from the real railroads:

4. Passenger trains must make a station stop for as long as it takes to count to 60 on every second trip around the oval.

The advantage of this rule was to let freights and switchers start a move or

two before having to wait for another trip of the passenger train at some congested junction or switch. Both trains were actually going most of the time with the new rule.

By this time a month had passed and we'd forgotten all about wanting a bigger railroad. Our little 4 x 8-foot layout was a lot bigger than we'd realized, considering all that could be done with it.

Other operating possibilities were in the realm of the "way freight." This is a local freight train that goes from factory to factory, into quarries, mines, team tracks (where transfer is made from trucks), and warehouses. The train may take "all day" picking up cars and setting others out. Then it goes to the yard with all the cars it has picked up and starts out, perhaps the next day, with another string to set out.

You can operate a way freight your-

Before: 3½'x6'

Fig. 5-1 (above). Instead of outgrowing a small table railroad, you can "grow" it a little bigger or make it the beginning of a large pike. This formed-plastic railroad terrain is typical of the smallest HO railroads. Fig. 5-2 (at right above) is a straight-down view. Fig. 5-3 (at right) shows some ways in which any simple railroad can be cut and spread to improve both trackage and scenery. The severed sections can be rejoined with wood framing.

After: 4½'x7'

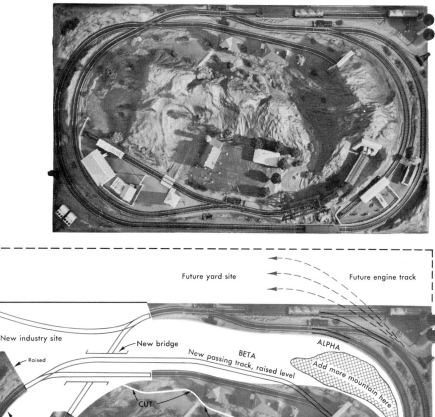

Future yard site

Future engine track

New industry site

New bridge

BETA

ALPHA

Raised

New passing track, raised level

Add more mountain here

CUT

CUT

Newly raised level

New switches

Future gorge and trestle site

DELTA

New industry site

GAMMA

New passing track

"Grow" your railroad

self or with the help of a conductor-brakeman to throw switches and signal when to back the engine, etc. Some men use shuffled cards to show where to put cars. Then a lot of the fun comes in figuring out how to switch each car in the fewest moves.

While all this operation was developing, we began to get other ideas. We started to build a working cable car — a funicular — such as you see in Los Angeles, Colorado resorts, Dubuque, Pittsburgh, and in the Swiss Alps. Usually one car goes up and the other down at the same time. See Fig. 5-4.

Meanwhile, I assembled many car kits, bought a few ready-made cars, and built two locomotives. Both boys assembled a few kits, too. We built extra houses, stores, and other buildings and we changed them

around from time to time for different effects.

Paul liked wiring especially, and soon he was working with only a little help from me on a way of controlling the train from the end of a long cord. It had two pushbuttons on the end: one made the train gradually increase speed; the other was a gradual brake. If you wanted an emergency stop, you pushed both buttons.

This kind of thing is beyond most model railroaders. Not because they can't do it, for Paul had had no previous electrical experience, but because you need a certain amount of extra personal interest in any craft to give you the patience that is always required for some parts of the job. Few model railroaders have that much patience in electrical things, so in this book I'll keep the wiring as simple as possible to accomplish the results I feel are basic for any small two-train

railroad. No pushbutton, walk-around control for us in this book.

Well, anyway, you can see my main point, that you don't have to keep adding track to have fun with a small railroad.

Larger railroads

Many model railroaders hope for the day when they can start a larger railroad. I mean a model railroad with about 150 square feet of surface. With this much space you can emphasize any phase of model railroading you wish and still have a little room for the rest of a complete railroad. You may prefer a really big yard and roundhouse if you like building, or at least collecting, cars and locomotives. Or if you like scenery more than anything else, you can keep the yard small and devote a large part of the space to mountains or other scenes. Many veteran model railroaders devote the larger part of their railroads

Fig. 5-4. Some model railroaders like to shift from one thing to another, keeping several projects going. Here on the railroad in the author's basement a cable car (funicular) is in early construction stages. A gap at the base of the cliff shows where scenery that was too close to the track was sawed away and will soon be replaced. A through-type bridge on a curve was too narrow to pass long cars and is being replaced by a deck girder bridge.

to a branchline operation, sometimes with trolley or narrow-gauge equipment, usually with "oldtime" cars and locomotives that are full of personality.

If you prefer railroadlike operation, you can forget appearance and use the space to wind several layers of track into a very long main line. Then you can operate trains several at a time, using all the railroad rules you can remember — plus a timetable and maybe a dispatcher. Or you can go to the other extreme and have the whole railroad run automatically.

Of course, you don't have to specialize. You can build just a larger but well-balanced railroad in any space.

If you'd like to specialize in more than one thing—many mountains plus a big yard, for instance—you'll probably need nearly double the space, perhaps 200 square feet or more. The more features of railroading that you want to emphasize, the more space you'll need.

Unfortunately, the bigger you plan, the more unlikely you will be to get the railroad in good working order. A model railroad can be too big — so big you can't keep up with it. How big it is depends on you — how much you can do, how much time you have, how much you will build yourself or buy ready to use, and how well you can build things so they don't need much adjusting or repairing. If you're a teenager, you may have only a few years left to build this railroad. You'll probably pick up model railroading stronger than ever later on, but during the years just after high school (being in the service, or perhaps getting married), you'll do less model railroading unless you have a very lucky situation. So don't set your sights too high.

Growing a railroad

There is an excellent way to build a railroad that I think is more fun, now that I've tried it, than to build the usual way.

The usual way is to build a table or framework, then all the track, then all the wiring, meanwhile buying or building cars and locomotives. After the track is running well, you start the scenery. When the scenery's done, you've rushed through the very part of the hobby that gives you the most fun. You may feel a sort of letdown and either think the hobby has no more to offer you, or else feel you must start another railroad. (An exception to this is the fellow who likes train operation best; he's less likely to tire of a completed railroad.)

I think the weak points of this plan are in two things: first, completing the track all at once; second, waiting to start the scenery. If you like track-building, you'll get done too soon and

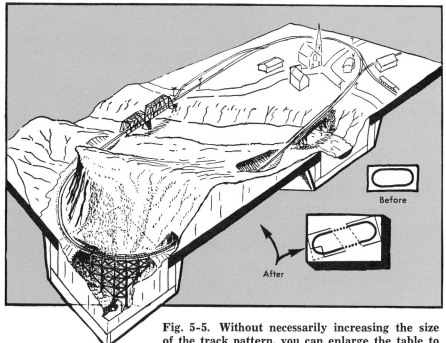

Fig. 5-5. Without necessarily increasing the size of the track pattern, you can enlarge the table to make more space for scenery. Note cocked angle of track, cut-away corner, and depressed river.

then the fun is over. If you don't like track-building, you may have so much of it to do that you bog down.

I suggest that you let your railroad grow gradually. Complete sections here and there rather than all over at once. If more fellows would follow this plan, there would be more model railroads that reach the scenery stage.

To grow a railroad, you start out with the same general plan as before. It may be in your head or carefully worked out on paper, whichever is the most fun. Then you build some of the track, perhaps the entire main line but with many of the switches and extra tracks left out. It's very easy to cut them in later on. With this approach you get some trains running right away, probably within a month of when you started building the bench or tablework.

Now with this mere skeleton of the future railroad, you begin to fill in. Build a little completed scenery here, an extra track there; add some of the yard tracks, some houses and factories. It's a mighty good idea to rough in all the scenic terrain. Scenery is so simple and cheap to build that there's no harm done if you change your mind later and tear out big hunks of it to rebuild a different way. You're a sort of sculptor creating the railroad gradually, a little here and a little there. You'll have a good-looking, well-operating railroad in short order, but it won't get big too fast. At any time parts of it will be sufficiently finished to show friends or take pictures, but you'll always have more you can build in any order you wish.

The best advice I can give you if this idea of growing the railroad appeals to you is this: Don't be the least afraid to take a saw and chisel to remove any part of the track, scenery, or even the tabletop and frame. It's easy to remove and easy to fill in again with another track or scenic arrangement. In this way your railroad can be changing continually. You'll be less likely to get tired of the pike, for it will never have to be finished.

Here are some examples of what you can do: Cut a slot across the tabletop to build a sunken riverbed. Of course, you fill in the gaps in the track with bridges (Fig. 5-5). Move the leg back and you can cut off a corner of the table so the curve of a track overhangs. Then build a gully below and a curved trestle to support the track. Saw along both sides of a level track and raise it up like a ramp to reach an elevated mine or to begin an upper level. Likewise, you can saw along the side of a track and move it sideways (Fig. 5-3). These things look drastic but they're often less work and more fun than to tear up track and lay it again.* Add shelves and extensions along the sides of the table to get extra space for track and scenery. Shorten the table legs or raise them for a more interesting viewing angle. Sometimes you can improve operation by tilting the whole tabletop an inch or so to favor a bad grade, introducing only a slight grade somewhere else in the process.

*A portable electric saber saw makes building and rebuilding a model railroad especially easy. I use a Stanley, but there are one or two other good makes. Some cut too slowly or break blades too often.

Project suggestions for the future

Add station platform, lights too.

Add highway crossing and flasher.

Build steps up steep bank or hill.

Sink cinder pit between rails.

Rebuild worst square foot of your pike.

Cut quarry into hillside.

Add L-shaped table wing for industries.

Add hinged extension to drop out of way.

Arrange flower beds at station, park.

Add mail crane.

Install working semaphore at junction.

Build section of "abandoned" roadbed.

Add telephone and power line poles.

Build ravine and culvert under tracks.

Build buildings up a hillside.

Add row of poplar trees along fence.

Add miniature figures in all occupations.

Put small birds on roofs and wires.

Add weeds to grass areas.

Build house on fire with firemen.

Add millpond, boat, ducks, mill.

Add elevated highway and bridge.

Put lights, seats, curtains in cars.

Add weight to plastic cars.

Put planks in grade crossing.

Add overhead footbridge.

Build fire escape on school, stores.

Add a dead tree in live row.

Carve eroded rivulets in plaster bank of hill.

Carve rock formations in cliff.

Redo grass areas with more texture, using several shades of color.

Experiment with different types of couplers.

Add wiring to couple on a helper engine at the base of a grade.

Add detail to locomotives.

Paint passenger cars and locos, stations, and signs a color scheme chosen for your own road.

Add a short trolley line.

Build a special shape track switch.

Add telltale at bridges and tunnels.

Give cars and buildings a weathered paint finish. This is one of the easiest and best ways to improve the whole effect.

This night scene on E. L. Moore's Elizabeth Valley RR. points out what can be accomplished with a few evenings of detail work. Some of the town of Elizabethtown's senior citizens are just relaxing in front of the saloon, but the crewmen in the background are tending to their chores of watering a switcher. Notice the lighted station with its interior detail, the poles along the street, the deep wagon tracks, and the signs on the buildings.

There is always room for people on a model railroad. G. C. Ketler of Pennsylvania has six men in this active scene on his Iron Ridge & Mayville RR.

Farms, stores, houses and other buildings not directly related to the railroad improve the over-all effect of the scene. Emmet Higgins did this job.

John Collins.

The 5 x 9-foot pike of Anthony Steitzel and his son Al is made up of a number of scenes, each of which contains many small details. Most of the equipment on the railroad came as kits, but by combining kits and adding some scratchbuilt parts, the Steitzels have created areas that look complete. Take this oil refinery, for instance: Six kits were used in addition to cigar tubes to represent the narrow tanks. Four other tanks, made of mailing tubes covered with rivet-embossed paper, also form part of the refinery. The stock facilities in the foreground were built to fit the narrow space between street and tracks. The cattle add life to the scene.

A skillful combination of kit and scratchbuilt equipment is evident on Karl Naffin's Lake Erie Line in Maple Heights, Ohio. The maintenance shack is a Revell product; the switcher on the trestle is the Mantua "Big Six" with scratchbuilt tender. The grain elevator and other buildings in the background were built from scratch.

One of those evenings when you don't quite know what to do with yourself, and you don't feel like getting involved in a major project on the railroad, try adding some trees, weeds and shrubs. This is a project that can be dropped anytime and is great for just passing time.

Boyce Martin has been busy with lichen, twigs and weeds and has used them liberally on his Nawsuh, Yewall & Shonuff RR., a branch line. Notice the vinelike weeds along the top of the rocks and the heavy growth beneath the trestle. This is the bluegrass country of Kentucky.

HO TRACK SECTIONS

with American-type rail joiners and rail.

Height of track: Atlas, Fleischmann, Tru-Track ______ 11/64″
Rivarossi and flexible track ________ 9/64″
Tru-Scale (includes ballast board) __ 13/32″

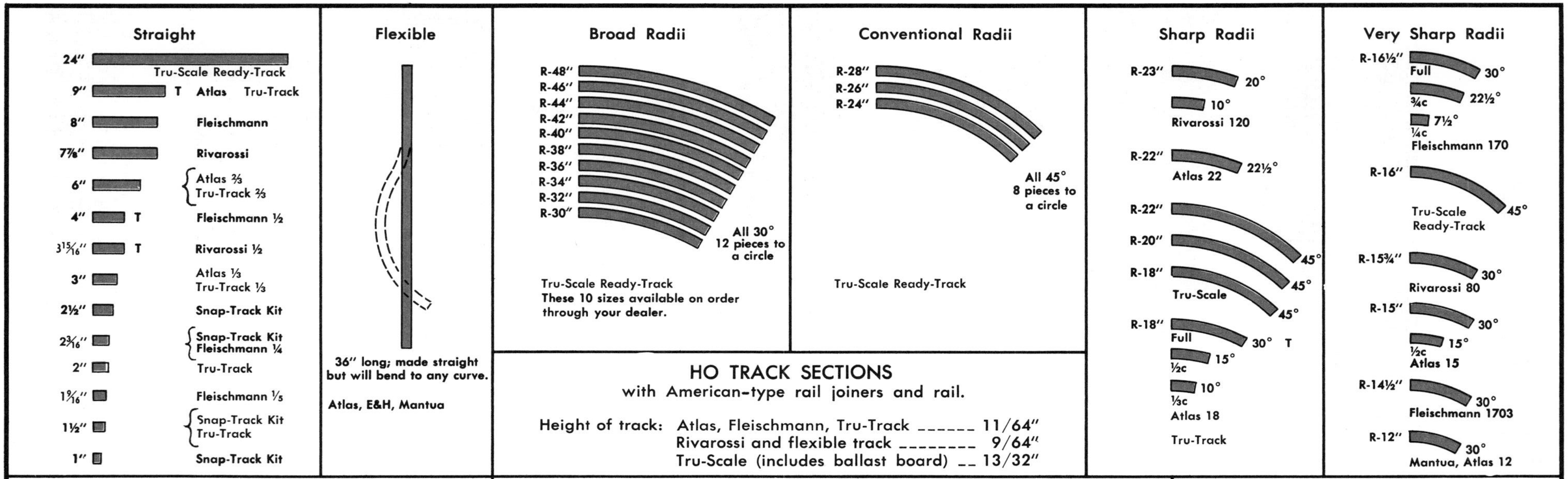

Straight
24″ Tru-Scale Ready-Track
9″ T Atlas Tru-Track
8″ Fleischmann
7⅞″ Rivarossi
6″ Atlas ⅔ Tru-Track ⅔
4″ T Fleischmann ½
3 15/16″ T Rivarossi ½
3″ Atlas ⅓ Tru-Track ⅓
2½″ Snap-Track Kit
2 3/16″ Snap-Track Kit Fleischmann ¼
2″ Tru-Track
1 9/16″ Fleischmann ⅕
1½″ Snap-Track Kit Tru-Track
1″ Snap-Track Kit
Flexible
36″ long; made straight but will bend to any curve.
Atlas, E&H, Mantua
Broad Radii
R-48″ R-46″ R-44″ R-42″ R-40″ R-38″ R-36″ R-34″ R-32″ R-30″
All 30° 12 pieces to a circle
Tru-Scale Ready-Track
These 10 sizes available on order through your dealer.
Conventional Radii
R-28″ R-26″ R-24″
All 45° 8 pieces to a circle
Tru-Scale Ready-Track
Sharp Radii
R-23″ 20°
10°
Rivarossi 120
R-22″ 22½°
Atlas 22
R-22″ R-20″ R-18″ 45° 45° 45°
Tru-Scale
R-18″ Full 30° T
½c 15°
⅓c 10°
Atlas 18
Tru-Track
Very Sharp Radii
R-16½″ Full 30°
¾c 22½°
¼c 7½°
Fleischmann 170
R-16″ 45°
Tru-Scale Ready-Track
R-15¾″ 30°
Rivarossi 80
R-15″ 30°
½c 15°
Atlas 15
R-14½″ 30°
Fleischmann 1703
R-12″ 30°
Mantua, Atlas 12

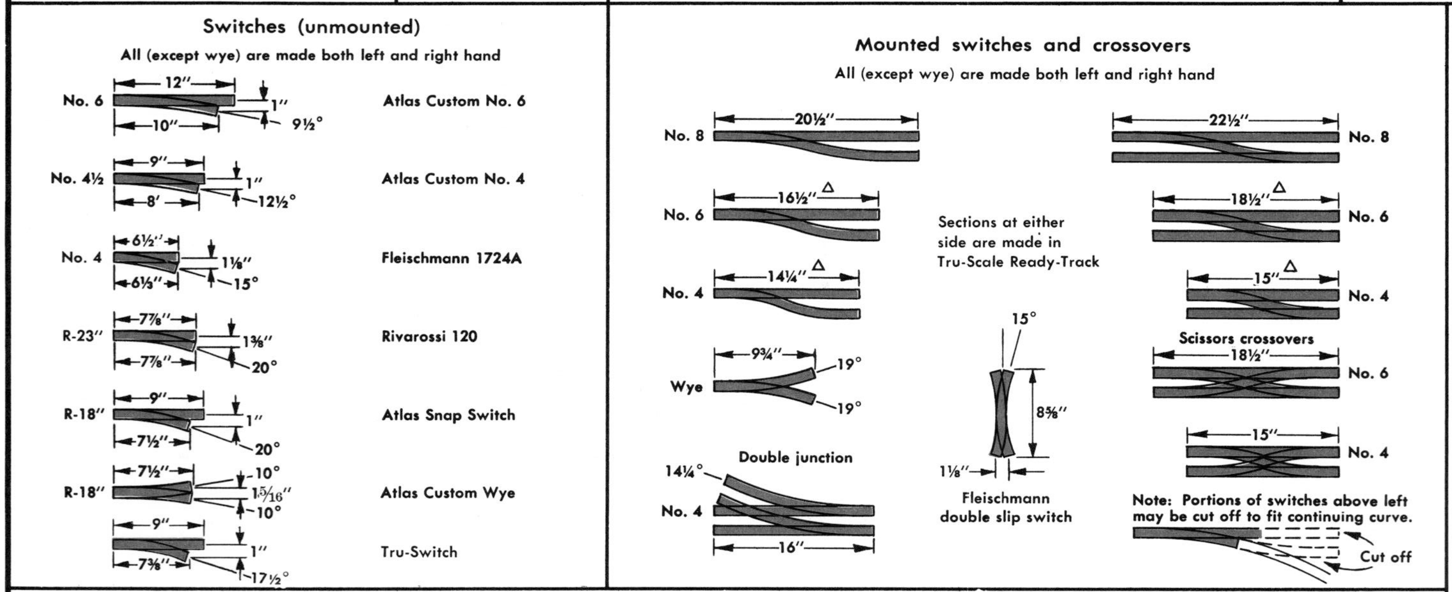

Switches (unmounted)
All (except wye) are made both left and right hand
No. 6 12″ 10″ 1″ 9½° Atlas Custom No. 6
No. 4½ 9″ 8′ 1″ 12½° Atlas Custom No. 4
No. 4 6½″ 6⅓″ 1⅛″ 15° Fleischmann 1724A
R-23″ 7⅞″ 7⅞″ 1⅜″ 20° Rivarossi 120
R-18″ 9″ 7½″ 1″ 20° Atlas Snap Switch
R-18″ 7½″ 10° 1 5/16″ 10° Atlas Custom Wye
9″ 7⅜″ 1″ 17½° Tru-Switch
Mounted switches and crossovers
All (except wye) are made both left and right hand
No. 8 20½″
No. 6 16½″ △
No. 4 14¼″ △
Wye 9¾″ 19° 19°
Double junction 14¼° No. 4 16″
22½″ No. 8
18½″ △ No. 6
15″ △ No. 4
Scissors crossovers 18½″ No. 6
15″ No. 4
Sections at either side are made in Tru-Scale Ready-Track
15° 8⅝″ 1⅛″
Fleischmann double slip switch
Note: Portions of switches above left may be cut off to fit continuing curve.
Cut off

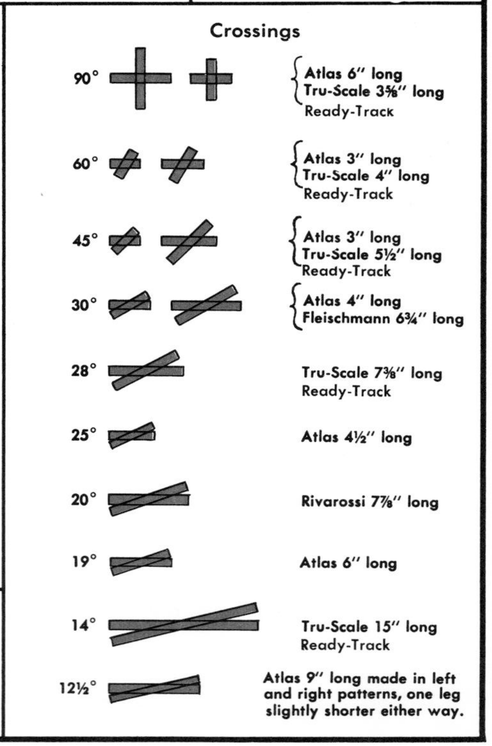

Crossings
90° Atlas 6″ long Tru-Scale 3⅝″ long Ready-Track
60° Atlas 3″ long Tru-Scale 4″ long Ready-Track
45° Atlas 3″ long Tru-Scale 5½″ long Ready-Track
30° Atlas 4″ long Fleischmann 6¾″ long
28° Tru-Scale 7⅜″ long Ready-Track
25° Atlas 4½″ long
20° Rivarossi 7⅞″ long
19° Atlas 6″ long
14° Tru-Scale 15″ long Ready-Track
12½° Atlas 9″ long made in left and right patterns, one leg slightly shorter either way.

T — These sections also available with electric terminal connections. Individual terminal clips are also made.
R — Radius of curve or curve through switch.
No. — Frog number of railroad-type switch.
△ — These mounted switches and crossovers are available with built-in remote control; they are then 15″ and 18½″ long for No. 4 and No. 6 respectively.
Insulated gap sections, uncoupling sections and bumpers are made by the various manufacturers to fit their track.

6: All about sectional track

HO track comes in many different lengths and different curve radii. This gives a great deal of flexibility when you design track patterns of your own, and it's all the simpler because the track of different manufacturers can be mixed to take advantage of a very wide variety of sizes. The opposite page shows the wide variety and you'll also notice "flexible track" listed. This deserves special comment. Also see Fig. 6-3.

Flexible track comes in 24" or 36" lengths and consists of the two rails clipped to a strip of ties. You can use this as a piece of straight track of any shorter length; it is easy to cut. You can buy separate rail joiners and you'll find they will join both flexible track and sectional track, so you can combine both types.

But the biggest advantage of flexible track isn't apparent unless the dealer demonstrates it. You can bend it to any curve easily in your hands. Thus you can get curves more gradual or sharper or the same as those of the regular track sections. This flexibility is very handy for all types of layout building.

When you bend a curve, one rail will be out of line with the other at the ends of the track, so you cut the longer rail back until it comes opposite to the shorter rail. Use a razor saw.

You can buy supplies to spike your own rails, but I don't recommend hand-laid track for beginning model railroaders. It is easy to set a bad car aside until you can fix it, but out-of-gauge track can upset the whole railroad until it's fixed. If you think you'd like to try track laying, you'll learn about it in the sequel to this primer, *Practical Guide to Model Railroading.*

Using sectional track

Sectional track has rail joiners at each end located on the right-hand rail as you point the track toward you. This allows you to join sections turned either way around in any order. When you push sections together or pull them apart, keep the track in line so you don't accidentally bend the rail joiners.

Extra rail joiners come in strips or in boxes, and you should keep a supply on hand. You can remove the rail joiners from sectional track as explained under the photos.

You can fasten sectional track to the table or to roadbed board with either glue, glue-ballast mix, or small nails. For track nails get ½" No. 18 flathead

Fig. 6-1. Atlas Snap-Track, Atlas Custom-Line Track, Tru-Scale Tru-Track and Fleischmann Supertrack (shown) are very similar. Metal rails slide into cleats that are molded into the tops of the plastic ties. Holes are provided in tie centers for fastening track to table with ½" No. 18 flathead nails or No. 0 screws. To remove rail joiners on Atlas, spread slightly, then pull hard. On the Fleischmann type, bend up the rear tabs of the joiner, then pull.

Fig. 6-2. Another type of Atlas track uses staples to hold rails to the ties. Both cleats and staples are used on switches. To remove anchored rail joiner, either loosen staple at the left, or else file off the rear end of joiner under the rail. With either type of track you can change the curves for special work by cutting the plastic under one rail between ties and bending the track to a new curve. Use a razor saw to cut plastic, also to cut rail for special lengths.

Fig. 6-3. Flexible track by Atlas, Tru-Scale and others consists of metal rails stapled to a fiber or plastic "tie strip." It can be used interchangeably with sectional track. You can cut it to any length you wish (with razor saw). You can bend it to any curve. After bending, trim the rail ends with the saw. Gaps in the material under the rails allow this bending. Be sure to buy extra metal rail joiners when you cut any kind of track to special lengths.

Fig. 6-4. Rivarossi track is similar in many ways to Atlas and Fleischmann track, but has fiber ties instead of plastic. Metal runners under the ties have tabs that reach up through holes in ties to hold rail. All the track shown on this page can be intermixed to take advantage of combining the various sizes shown on the opposite page. If rail of any kind is slightly higher than another, file it down to match at the rail joint.

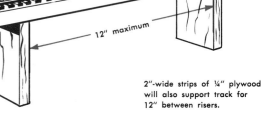

Use layers of cardboard to gradually raise track about ¼″ to join roadbed. Put longest card on top, short pieces below it.

Fig. 6-6.

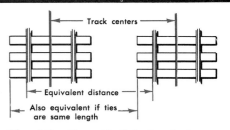

Elevated track on wood roadbed will support itself on spans up to 12″ long.

Fig. 6-7.

2″-wide strips of ¼″ plywood will also support track for 12″ between risers.

Fig. 6-5. Tru-Scale Ready-Track is a very firm type of sectional track that comes ready-laid on ballast board with special paint that simulates the gravel sides of the ballast. The track can be sawed to special lengths with a razor saw; if your saw is too narrow to go clear through from the top, turn the piece over to saw through the wood. This track is about ¼″ higher than types without ballast board; it can be joined to them easily if you shim the lower track upward (Fig. 6-6). All roadbed-track can be self-supporting for distances up to 12″, as in Fig. 6-7. Other types can be supported on plywood.

nails. If the track doesn't have holes already in the ties, you can drill them with a pin vise and small drill. (See the tools chapter.) One nail per track section is usually enough. Don't pound the nails quite all the way down. Then you can remove them when you want to change track around. Temporary track arrangements can be anchored by using masking tape at the ends of the ties to hold the track in place.

Good practice

You can lay track in any arrangement you wish, but here are some things that are considered good practice:

TRACK CENTERS: Parallel lines of *straight* track are usually spaced 2″ apart, center to center. In a pinch you can reduce this to 1¾″ if you don't have to get your fingers down between cars on adjacent tracks. Wider spacing is often convenient to accommodate poles, signals, station platforms between tracks, or to join curves.

DOUBLE-TRACK CURVES: When yards or double-track lines come to a curve, the track spacing must be increased so cars and engines on adjacent tracks won't sideswipe. Short cars and locos, such as you might start out with, are not likely to give trouble, and for this very reason it is easy to start a railroad with tracks too close together. But if you use the following table as a guide, you'll find almost every piece of equipment that can stay on the sharp curved track will not sideswipe equipment on the next track.

Radius	Spacing to next track
15″ to 18″	3″
18″ to 24″	2½″
24″ to 30″	2¼″
30″ and up	2″

How track is measured

STRAIGHT TRACK. There is no standard length for a piece of straight track, but the most common piece is 9″ long. A ⅓ section usually refers to one 3″ long. It is safer to figure in inches throughout. Our table shows the sizes both ways.

CURVED TRACK. Most HO track is cut 12 pieces to the circle, but some is 16 or other lengths. A practical but unfortunately little used way to indicate the amount of turn is by degrees, and our chart shows degrees of various sections. A full circle totals 360°.

RADIUS OF CURVATURE. The sharpness of curves is usually indicated by the radius. This is measured from the center of a circle to the center of the

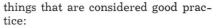

Center of circle

Radius

Rails

track, midway between the two rails.

TRACK CENTERS. This term refers to the spacing between parallel tracks (see above). The measurement is made from center to center of track, but if it is more convenient, you may measure from left rail to left rail, as this is the same distance.

SWITCH SIZE. Track switches for sharp curves have a circular curve that is of the same radius throughout.

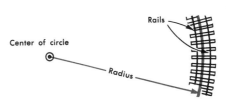

Track centers

Equivalent distance

Also equivalent if ties are same length

The Atlas Snap-Switch, for instance, has an 18″ radius curve. But larger switches and real railroad switches very often do not have a simple curve and cannot be described by radius. The curve of the switch may actually have some lengths of straight track along it. These switches are then numbered according to the angle of the frog. A No. 4 switch is almost as sharp as the Snap-Switch, while a No. 8 is so long that most model railroads haven't space for it.

FROG NUMBER. This is a simple way of measuring the angle between rails at the frog where they cross in

How to lay glue-ballast

Diluted glue
(see caption)

Fig. 6-8. Ballast solidified with thinned white glue makes a realistic and practical way to hold track in place. Use nails only until the glue has set. Brush small-size ballast into the "prismoidal shape" seen on real railroads. Get it between ties but not against the inside of rails. Now mix about 1 part white glue with 6 parts water and add a few drops of liquid detergent per quart of mix. The detergent makes the water spread everywhere when you apply the glue just inside the rails between ties; see sketch. The right amount of glue will hold the track firmly but will still allow you to break away the track or the ballast for track changes in the future. Remove any loose ballast with a vacuum cleaner. Fiber ties warp in water solutions, but the same method can be used with fiber ties using thinned model cement.

---

a switch. Lay a ruler across the rails at some point near the frog that is just one small unit across. For instance, find the point where the rails spread just ¼". Then turn the ruler and see how many of the same units run from this place to the point of the

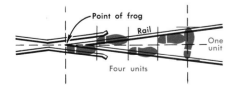

frog. If it is four times as far, you have a No. 4 switch or a No. 4 frog. In making this second measurement, lay the ruler midway between the rails, not along one of them. You can find the frog number of real railroad switches in this same way by using the length of your foot as a measure.

FROG ANGLE. This is just another way of measuring the size of the frog and it's done in degrees. A No. 6 frog happens to have an angle of 9½ degrees, while a No. 4 should have an angle of 14¼ degrees. However, Atlas "No. 4" switches in HO are actually made with 12½-degree angles, which really makes them No. 4½. This difference was made to provide a switch that would fit other sectional track more conveniently.

SCALE MILE. This is ⅟87 of a real mile in HO and is 60 feet (more exactly, 60.69 feet). A loco going 1 foot a second is going about 60 scale miles per hour.

PER CENT OF GRADE. This is the rise of track in 100 units of distance. For instance, if you use ¼" for a unit, than a rise of ¾" in 25" would be 3 units in 100 or 3 per cent. A 3 per cent grade is common in HO.

ELEVATION. The elevation of track is usually shown only on plans where the track goes up and down hill. It indicates the height from some zero place to the track level somewhere else. Usually the lowest place in the track is taken as zero and measurements are made to the top of the roadbed where the ties will rest. However, real railroads measure to the base of the rail (top of ties), and you can choose any place that's convenient as long as all measurements are made that same way.

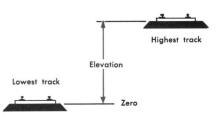

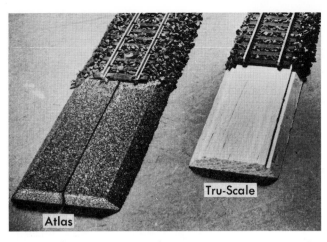

Fig. 6-9. Roadbed board (Tru-Scale) or cork (Atlas) with sloping shoulders improves the realism of the railroad.

Fig. 6-11. Long cars and engines have so much overhang that they may not be able to negotiate reverse curves unless you put at least 9″ of straight track between.

Notice that the popular idea that double track can be spaced 2″ between centers on curves is hardly ever good practice.

When curves sharper than 15″ radius are used, any general rule could be too misleading. This is because only certain kinds of railroads, such as interurban lines, are likely to use long cars or engines on such sharp curves. Here it is a good idea to try your longest pieces of equipment before locating any track permanently.

CURVE RADII: Selection of radii for curves is a tug of war between the need for sharp curves, to get more railroad into a space, and broad curves, to get the best performance. In general it is better to use curves of 24″ or more radius wherever you can. This is one place where flexible track is handy. All HO locomotives should be able to run on 24″ radius curves. Full-length passenger cars also can run on 24″ curves, but look best on 30″ or greater radius.

For most fellows, 30″ and sometimes 24″ curves take too much space, but it is usually best to use the largest radius you can.

The end curves of a table railroad usually determine how sharp you must go. For instance, a table 48″ wide could use curves of 22″ radius but not 24″ because you not only must double the radius, but also add something for the width of a track, about 2″, to get the total width of an oval track plan.

Often the extra space taken by switches at the ends of curves will limit the radius still more, 18″ usually being the most suitable radius for use on a table 4 feet wide.

Most cars and engines are advertised as being able to go around 18″ radius, but for some of the larger units this is more a stunt than a practicality. When you allow for imperfections in both equipment and track, there are many locos and some cars that are far better off on 22″ radius.

These include longer steam locomotives like Pacifics and Mikados, long passenger diesels, and long electric locomotives like the Pennsylvania GG-1. All of these will actually run on 18″ radius oval track, but may not do as well on a railroad including Snap-Switches and changes of grade near the switches unless you put a little skill into getting the track and wheels into perfect shape.

In general, I'd say the recommended limits of equipment for various curves should be something like this:

80-foot passenger cars	24″ up
Articulated locomotives	24″ up
Long passenger diesels	22″ up
Pacifics, Mikados (with exceptions)	22″ up
Large-wheel electrics	22″ up
Other locos and cars except as below	18″ up
Short 8-wheel diesels and electrics	14″ up
6-wheel steam switchers	14″ up
Interurban cars	12″ up
Ordinary freight cars	9″ up
4-wheel cars and engines and streetcars	6″ up

It is quite likely, as with Penn Line, Fleischmann, and Rivarossi engines, that future designs will be able to take tighter curves, for that has been a steady trend in HO. Years ago 24″ was the sharpest radius we allowed.

REVERSE CURVES: When you have two long curves joined together in an S fashion, try to include a piece of full-length straight track, 9″ or so, between the reversed curves. This will reduce the chance of derailments due to couplers not lining up or due to sudden swings of wheels under locomotives.

Track support

Most model railroads are built on a plywood surface or on strips of plywood supported on a frame. While it adds to the cost, adding a ½″ layer of "Homasote" is well worth while. This makes an ideal work surface, lets you use ⅜″ instead of ½″ plywood, and deadens noise. Yard tracks can be laid directly on it. Some lumberyards carry this material.

Main tracks on a real railroad line are usually raised a little and your railroad will look more impressive if you raise main lines on some sort of

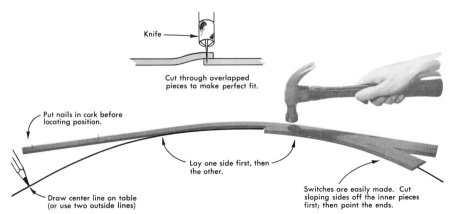

Fig. 6-10. Like flexible track, cork roadbed will bend to any curve arrangement. Foam plastic roadbed is similar but it comes in one part instead of in halves and it has special turnout pieces. Lay cork roadbed as shown here.

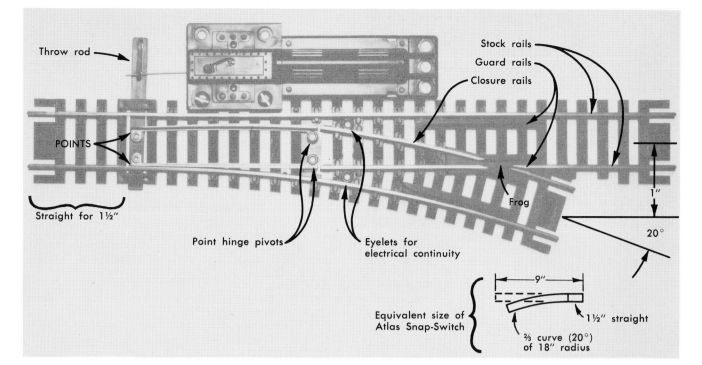

Throw rod

POINTS

Straight for 1½"

Point hinge pivots

Eyelets for electrical continuity

Stock rails

Guard rails

Closure rails

Frog

1"

20°

Equivalent size of Atlas Snap-Switch

9"

⅔ curve (20°) of 18" radius

1½" straight

Fig. 6-12. Parts of Atlas Snap-Switch.

"roadbed," Fig. 6-9. One popular type is made from soft pinelike wood. Tru-Scale roadbed is made two ways; one type is with milled ties in the top for those who lay their own rails. But if you use sectional track, get plain roadbed without ties.

The wood can be sawed easily to fit any curves you wish to lay. Radii are available in several sizes and you can combine short lengths to get intermediate curves.

Fleischmann makes a handy curvable foam plastic ballast.

Atlas roadbed is made of cork. You split it apart and lay one half along a line (Fig. 6-11), then the other half. It bends to any curve and is easily cut for any kind of fitting with a modeler's knife. Use flathead No. 18 nails for both the ballast strips and the track; ½" long is ample.

To give the ballast board a final touch, add a layer of glue-ballast, again as in Fig. 6-8, but this time the basic shape is already made for you.

Supporting upper-level track

When you want track to rise above the table level, you can use sets of piers made by Atlas, Revell, Authenticast, Ideal, and others for a trestle effect. Too much of this can look toylike, so much of your upper-level track should eventually be surrounded with plaster scenery, as though on elevated ground. Wood strips at least 2" wide can also be used for upper levels. To avoid sagging, use vertical risers or other supports under elevated roadbed with the following spacings:

Supporting material — 2" wide or more	Spacing between supports — absolute maximum
⅛" hardboard	7"
¼" plywood	12"
Tru-Scale roadbed	12"
⅜" plywood	16"
½" plywood	24"
¾" plywood	36"
1" lumber on its side	36"

Notice that Tru-Scale roadbed is self-supporting between the risers. On the other hand, materials like Celotex or cork must have additional support at all points.

Track switches

Switches are just as effective as locomotives in creating fun on the model railroad. Eventually you'll want quite a few switches, but you can add them gradually as traffic requires. Fortunately, HO switches are not expensive and you can buy most makes one at a time instead of in pairs. Remote control is available for all switches and you can also add "switch machines" to a manual switch to convert it to remote control.

When you use switches in your

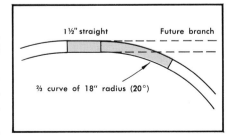

1½" straight   Future branch

⅔ curve of 18" radius (20°)

Fig. 6-13. When you lay track, the combination of 1½" straight plus a ⅔ section of 18" radius curve can be fitted to any place where you would like to add a Snap-Switch later on.

track plan, you'll find they won't always fit where you'd like them to. Switches usually take up more space and must be placed farther apart than you might think. The lengths and other dimensions of switches are shown on the chart, page 18. Use it as a general aid in figuring out what you can do, but this doesn't mean you have to do any arithmetic to work out a track plan. If you prefer, you can just lay out the track in various ways until it fits. If you don't have all the track you need, make some full-size paper copies of sample pieces of track and work out the track plan with the paper track.

Make your paper copies or "templates" by laying a sheet over the rails and rubbing the paper with a crayon.

Future switches — caution

For an example of why switches won't often fit in the same space as a piece of plain curved track, consider the dimensions of the Atlas Snap-Switch. Although Snap-Switches are made to be used with curves of 18" radius, they have a length of 1½" permanently straight ahead of the points (Fig. 6-12). For this reason, you cannot just remove a length of 18" curve and expect to fit a switch in its place. If you hope to add a switch into a curve at some future time, add a 1½" short "fitter" track at the site now (Fig. 6-13).

The Atlas Snap-Switch* is equal to a ⅔ length (20°) of 18" radius track plus 1½" of straight at the point end.

*Note that Atlas makes Snap-Switches in only one size, 18" radius. The other Atlas switches are Custom switches, sizes 4 and 6, although they are sometimes wrongly called Snap-Switches.

See small drawing in Fig. 6-12. In the same way, the Atlas No. 4 switch is about equivalent to a curve of 36″ radius and 12½° long.

Roughly speaking, the Snap-Switch limits your equipment to about 16″-radius-curve limitations, even though the actual curve is 18″ radius. Some train-set locomotives will not go through a switch this sharp unless everything is in perfect shape.

Fleischmann's No. 4 switch is approximately equivalent to a piece of 30″ radius track 15° long. Tru-Scale's No. 4 is about the same except that it has long ends that you can, and often should, trim off, depending on where you use it. Tru-Scale's Tru-Switch is about the same as a piece of 18″ radius track 20° long, with 1⅛″ of straight at the point end.

Rivarossi switches are about the same as a 22″ radius curve, but exactly match the Rivarossi 23″ radius track. Sometimes Rivarossi switches will fit where nothing else will.

When you have a very large space, size 6 or even size 8 turnouts are desirable because of their long prototypical look. On the other hand, size 4 will handle all cars and engines just as well and should usually be preferred, since they allow for equally important considerations such as better yard design, more side tracks, and more space for cars and scenery. It is not practical to use switches size 6 or larger in place of ordinary curves unless the entire curve is relaid.

7: Tracklaying kinks

I'VE already said quite a bit about fitting HO track sections and especially switches. In practice you'll have little trouble, especially since so many short lengths and different radii are available. But there are a few things you ought to know about if you want your railroad to perform well.

When joining sections of track permanently, leave a paper-thin gap between the ends of one track section and the next so the track will have room to expand a little the next time it gets warm. This will also allow wood tabletops to shrink a little in dry weather.

When you join sections, hold each piece of track in line and push the tracks straight together; otherwise you may kink the rail joiners. If you know where you will need insulated rail joiners for electrical blocks later on, you can put them in the track right away. If not, don't worry about it, for there are other easy ways to make the insulated joints.

Sometimes the end of a rail joiner is bent slightly and won't let the tracks come together. This can happen quite often, and you keep trying to put the track together and wondering why you are so clumsy about it.

Be sure joined tracks really line up, especially between any curved sections. It isn't easy to spot a kink at a rail joint in a curve unless you lay another piece of track of the same radius over two joined pieces to see how they line up (Fig. 7-1).

You can always bend track to fit a new alignment. One simple method is to undercut the plastic bridgework under the rails between ties and then slide the rails a little in their cleats to put a curve in straight track or to alter the curve of other track. Of course, you can buy flexible track with the bending provision already made for you. After bending the track, one rail will end up longer than the other, so trim it off with a razor saw and then dress the cut end smooth with a small file or fine abrasive cloth.

Cutting special lengths

The razor saw is also good for cutting tracks to a special length. You may have to do this when you tie a new line into an old plan. Lay the new track overlapping the place where it should join the old and saw right down through the lower track, or, in some cases, right through both pieces (Fig. 7-2). The block of wood shown beyond the upper piece of track in Fig. 7-2 is used to take up both the sideways push of the saw and the crosswise push of the rails while cutting.

After the cuts are made, you'll have to saw horizontally along the top of the first ties under each rail to make space for new rail joiners (Fig. 7-3).

How to make track sections fit

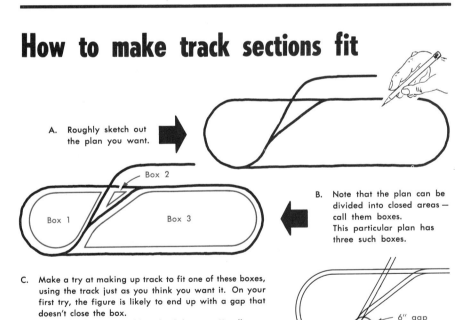

A. Roughly sketch out the plan you want.

B. Note that the plan can be divided into closed areas — call them boxes. This particular plan has three such boxes.

Box 1   Box 2   Box 3

6″ gap

6″ track

Gap now closes

C. Make a try at making up track to fit one of these boxes, using the track just as you think you want it. On your first try, the figure is likely to end up with a gap that doesn't close the box.

D. Notice the direction and length of the gap. Usually you can add a track of approximately this length at some other place (where the direction is right) to make the gap close the box. Sometimes it will require two pieces of track in two different places to make the box close itself. Pieces on the opposite side of the box will tend to increase the gap; on the near side they tend to make it overlap. Sometimes you do both in different amounts or directions.

E. Build each box before going on to another. It is a good idea to begin with the smallest box; for instance, Box 2 in B.

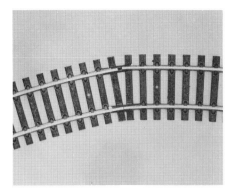

Fig. 7-1. Avoid kinked rail joints.

Fig. 7-2. Saw cuts through the track.

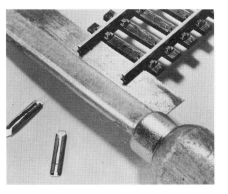

Fig. 7-3. Undercut for rail joiners.

Sometimes you'll want to take out a piece of track between others that should stay put. This is easily done, too. First, you saw right through the rail joiners at each end of the wanted track. Then you lift the old track out; often you can do this so neatly that the old piece can be used again.

When you drop new track in place, cut some rail joiners one-half to two-thirds as long as normal and push them all the way onto the ends of your new track. When the track is down in place, you can slide the short joiners out enough to hold the track firmly. This trick is also handy for track you may want to remove frequently — for instance, across a hinge line between the table and a drop-leaf addition or onto a drawbridge that's only occasionally opened.

Loose rail joiners may work out of place and will also be poor conductors of electricity. It helps to give them a little pinch (not too much) before slipping them onto a rail. Joiners should slide on easily but not loosely.

8: Track maintenance

ORDINARILY you'll have very little trouble with sectional track as long as you avoid kinks in the curves and wide gaps between sections. But sometimes track does get out of gauge and sometimes car wheels are out of gauge too. When the two combine, you have a derailment for sure. If many cars derail at the same place, the track is surely defective.

Get a track gauge at a hobby shop. (Make sure the gauge is correct, for some poor ones have been sold.) Lay the gauge on your track and slide it along. It will tend to bind when track isn't correct.

Now use some of the same kind of spikes that advanced model railroaders use to lay their own track and force the rail into the correct position. Spikes are driven first with needle-nose (chain-nose) pliers and then tapped home with a hammer and nail set (Fig. 8-1). You can drive the spikes between ties for convenience, or else drill holes through the ties for better appearance. Atlas ties have some holes already there.

If you spike only one rail down, you may merely shift the whole track, so it's necessary to spike both sides of both rails to make sure the gauge is corrected. If you spike outside both rails first, then inside, the gauge will be narrowed; and vice versa.

Switch maintenance

The serious track troubles are most likely to occur at switches, where rails can easily get out of gauge and where wheels find the most places to get fouled anyway. Here are things to look for in a troublesome switch:

1. See that the sharp ends of the switch points rest tightly against the stock rail on either side when thrown either way. If you don't know the

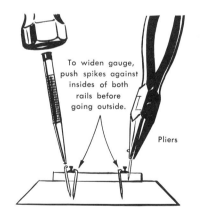

To widen gauge, push spikes against insides of both rails before going outside.

Pliers

Fig. 8-1. Be sure spikeheads won't touch wheel flanges. Heads must be at least .04" (about 3/64") below rail tops for correct American HO wheels. Some nonstandard wheels have flanges that will touch almost any spikes. On hand-spiked track, avoid such wheels.

names of these parts, see Fig. 6-12.

2. See that the point is also level with the top of the stock rail, each side again.

3. Check the gauge of the track all the way along the switch, especially on the curved side.

4. See that the hinge end of the switch point also lines up with the closure rail and almost meets it.

5. See if the weight of a train forces any part of the points out of correct position. This will take close observation in good light while the train moves slowly. Pulse power helps here.

On Atlas switches the closure rail may work its way forward and push against the points, preventing them from moving all the way to one or both sides. This rail can be tapped a little back toward the frog to correct this. If it won't move, touch a hot soldering iron to the pivot point of the switch for a second while you move the points against the stock rail. The heat will soften the plastic just enough to let the pivot move and clear the obstruction.

Often derailments occur at the point of the frog of Atlas switches. This can be eliminated by trimming this point a little blunter with a model knife. Also, be sure there is no twist or change of grade of the wood supporting any track switches.

9: Return-loop wiring

"WHEN the train crosses a switch, it stops." That's a comment I've often heard from fellows who are building their first railroad. Another complaint is that after a new track is added, none of the trains will run.

Such stalling may be due to faulty wiring or other causes of short or open circuits, but on a new railroad it is often because of a built-in short circuit in the track pattern itself. This kind of short circuit occurs if you don't add special wiring when you have a "return track" as shown in color in Fig. 9-1.

A return track is any place where a locomotive can be turned end-for-end. A turntable is an obvious example. But any track pattern where a route doubles back on itself is also a return track, or a turning track.

In each example of Fig. 9-1, a train can start at K and move to the right by a circuitous route, eventually getting back to K but facing the other way. K is the "key switch" and the loop of track marked in color behind this switch is the "return track." In turning, the train uses this track only once.

I shall refer to the track ahead of the key switch as "main line." This is the track the engine uses twice, both going in and coming out facing the other way. Soon we will create two electrical "direction districts" associated with the return track and the main track respectively.

All the return loops in Fig. 9-1, and those on your railroad as well, are really alike, but just stretched differently. In the case of the wye, part of the loop is a switchback, but electrically all return loops are the same, so here (Fig. 9-2) is a generalized diagram of any return track.

Use a slip of paper as a locomotive on this diagram. Mark the front of the loco, and also mark the right-hand wheels with a plus sign. (For *forward* operation, the right-hand wheels must be connected to electricity of positive polarity. The left wheels are negative.)

So, going into the loop, the S rail (south rail) must be positive. In the loop the RS rail must be positive. But look what happens coming out of the loop. Now the right-hand wheels will be on the N rail, so this rail must now be the one with plus polarity. If the N rail should remain negative, the engine would try to back up suddenly, or else the wheels would short-circuit across the insulated gaps near the switch.

Maybe you can guess what we've got to do now. We have to do it while the train is rounding the turning loop.

The wires connecting the main track must be reversed so the train can continue forward after rounding the loop. This is done by adding a "reversing switch" as shown in Fig. 9-3. This toggle is wired so that in one position the wires reach the S and N rails in the normal way, but when you flip the toggle lever the wires are interchanged as shown at the lower right. Thus, you can make either the S or the N rail the positive side.

Power from the toggle follows the two mainline rails through the track switch but cannot pass beyond the insulated rail gaps. You can call this toggle the "Mainline Direction Controller."

The rails beyond the gaps are the return track district and are powered by separate wires that must not pass through the mainline direction controller toggle. That's because we want the locomotive to continue around the loop without reversing when the mainline toggle is flipped.

Insulated rail gaps

Insulated rail joiners or gaps can be either purchased or homemade.

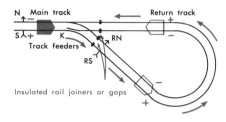

Fig. 9-2. Where to connect feeders.

You can get plastic rail joiners at the hobby shop to replace a metal rail joiner in each of the four rails somewhere behind the key switch, K. Or, if your track is already fastened down, it will be more convenient to saw completely through the rails with a razor saw. Then squirt a little Ambroid cement into the saw cut to prevent the rails from creeping together and closing the gap. When diagrams show gaps, you can use either the plastic joiners or the saw cuts, as you prefer.

Reversing switches

In Fig. 9-3, I've shown a toggle type of switch, but *any* kind of electrical switch can be substituted as long as it can carry 1 ampere or more and has *at least* two poles and two positions or "throws." The toggle shown is a double-pole double-throw (dp. dt.). The two wires cross-connecting diagonal corners must be added to the back of this switch to make it into a reversing switch.

Toggles come both plain and in a "center-off" variety which has the feature of an extra turned-off position when the handle is midway — an improvement you will usually want.

Some switches especially made for model railroading have the crossed wires built in. These are made by American Flyer, Rivarossi, Atlas and others. The Atlas Twin contains two such switches. See Fig. 9-5.

Practical loop circuit

In actual practice, it's better to have two of these direction-control switches as shown in Fig. 9-4. This makes the wiring for the main district and the loop district identical. It also simplifies operation when you want to go

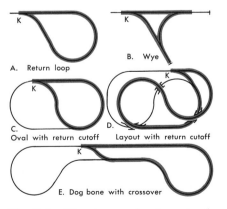

A. Return loop

B. Wye

C. Oval with return cutoff

D. Layout with return cutoff

E. Dog bone with crossover

Fig. 9-1. Five types of return track.

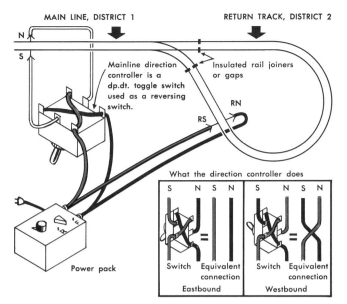

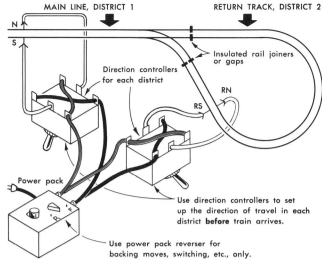

Fig. 9-3. Toggle switch is shown upside down for clarity.

Fig. 9-4. Two toggles allow for more flexible control.

around the loop in reverse direction.

To operate, use the two toggles as direction-control levers. These are a sort of "dispatcher's control." You never use them to reverse a train, unless it's at the end of a trip. You do use them to set up the direction of travel before a train gets into each direction district.

Suppose a train is approaching from the left. First you check the return district direction controller to see if it's set the way you want to go through the loop, clockwise or counterclockwise. Then, after the train has completely cleared the main line, you flip the main district's direction controller to reverse the polarity there. This is equivalent to flipping the toggle from eastbound to westbound operation.

The built-in reversing switch in the power pack is usually left in the same position, to the right or upward, as the case may be. You reverse it only for switching moves and at times when you want the locomotive to back a short distance. It is an "engineer's" rather than a dispatcher's control.

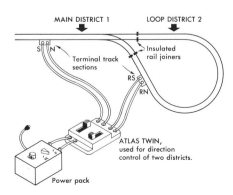

Fig. 9-5. How to use Atlas Twin units.

Where to put the gaps

Usually placing the district boundary gaps close behind the key switch is most convenient, but not always. If you want to put the return district gaps farther from the key switch on either or both branches for any reason, you may. The only limitation is that the return-track district remaining between the gaps be long enough to hold the longest train that will pass through.

The reason is that if the gaps are too close together, wheels at both ends of a train will be crossing gaps at the same time. One set of gaps is bound to be at a polarity mismatch and then any metal wheels crossing it will be pitted from momentary short circuits. This can also make trains jerk badly, or even stall completely.

To summarize, we use pairs of gaps to create two direction districts. One district will be entirely within a return track, and will be at least as long as the trains that will use it. Each district will be electrically separate and will have its own direction switch. All boundaries between districts will have gaps in both rails.

These direction districts are sometimes called sections but they should not be confused with "blocks." A block is used to isolate power to run two different trains and you don't need blocks on a one-train railroad. But if you have a return track, you need direction districts even if you run only one train. Later on you may divide the direction districts into smaller blocks for two-train operation.

Complicated trackage

Often two direction districts will connect to each other at three or more places. If there are additional ways to

get from the return district to the main district, each such route must also have gaps in both rails (Fig. 9-6). Again keep in mind that no train must cross a mismatched set of gaps at either end.

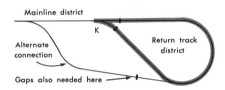

Fig. 9-6. Extra gaps sometimes needed.

On many track plans there are two or more return loops, wyes, or other turning track arrangements. A safe way to wire them is to create a new district for each turning track, adding as many direction controllers as needed. But in a moment I'll show you that you can get by more conveniently and with less expense using never more than three and usually only two direction controllers.

To find additional return tracks, get out that paper locomotive and a plan of your track again. Mark the gaps you have already provided.

Now see if you can still get the loco turned end for end, but without crossing the gaps that mark the existing district boundaries. If you can find another way to get the loco turned end for end you have found another return track.

You can treat this new return track the same way as the first, putting gaps in it to separate it into a third district and making sure all gaps are far enough apart that a train never crosses two sets at the same time. This would require three toggles in all for direction control.

But usually you can get by with only two direction control toggles and you *never* need more than three on a one-train railroad. You can cut the number needed by powering two or more return track districts (that don't join each other physically) through the same toggle. For instance, in the dogbone plan of Fig. 9-7, there are re-

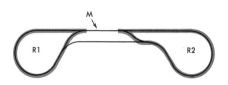

Fig. 9-7. Return loops at each end.

turn loops at each end, created by the two crossovers in the middle part of the plan. The obvious course is to create three districts, for R1, M and R2. But in Fig. 9-8, you'll see that only two districts are needed. By making one side of the "double track" part of the plan into one district and the other side into another district — that is, dividing the whole plan horizontally through the crossovers — two districts, M and R, will do the job.

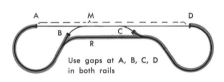

Fig. 9-8. Only two districts needed.

As for the location of gaps, a pair should be in the middle of the crossovers, but you have a lot of leeway with gaps A and D. A, for instance, can be moved to the right as long as a whole train can fit between A and C. Or A can be moved to the left and around the loop as long as there is still a train-length of space from A to B.

Gaps B and C might be closer to each other and a train could be crossing them both if it snaked through both crossovers at the same time. But here the gaps don't have to be separated by a train length because these two pairs of gaps will either be both matched or both mismatched at the same time. When they're both matched, train wheels can't cause any short circuits. So, here you can make an exception to the rule that district boundaries must be separated by a train length.

Hobby shop men will often check your wiring diagrams. If you're still not very sure about things, you can find a more fully illustrated discussion of return tracks in the book *How to Wire Your Model Railroad.*

C. W. Witbec

A type of steam switcher commonly seen on model railroads is the 0-6-0, such as No. 77 of the Southern Pacific Lines, above. Below is a similar engine of the HO scale Sunset Ry., built from a Roundhouse kit.

A. L. Schmid

Prototypes and models

This is a model of the American Locomotive Co. (Alco) road switcher, built from a Hobbytown kit. Road switchers are general-purpose locomotives used in passenger as well as local and through freight service.

Wallace W. Abbe

Thousands of F units have been built by the Electro-Motive Division of General Motors; they are in use all over the country. Models of the F are available from a number of manufacturers. The F is a freight unit.

This mighty articulated locomotive is the Union Pacific 4-8-8-4 "Big Boy." With two sets of drivers and two sets of cylinders it is actually two engines under one boiler. Such engines were fascinating to watch in action.

This sleek Pacific was one of B&O's President class P-7 series, named after the first 20 Presidents of the U. S. (except the second Adams). This is President Lincoln.

This is an Electro-Motive switcher, common on American railroads. Models are available from numerous makers.

The PRR GG-1 is a popular prototype among modelers of electric roads. A model is available from Penn Line.

Burdell L. Bulgrin.

A late EMD model is the GP-20. Models of this type of general-purpose motive power are available in HO.

The Mantua 2-8-2 is particularly appropriate for mainline freight trains. This kit model was built by the author.

10: Locomotives on the railroad

MORE THAN 100 different locomotives are available in HO. Many come ready to run; others come in kits; still others come both ways. It's a good idea to know how the different types of locos are used in real railroading before you make your selection.

Let's start with steam locomotive types. You can tell a lot about them just by looking first at the driving wheels and then at the smaller wheels in the pilot or leading truck and in the trailing truck. Many books show all the various kinds of wheel arrangement and give their names such as Atlantic, Pacific, etc., but I'll confine my remarks here to generalities.

In general, engines with large-diameter driving wheels are for fast service. Engines with many driving wheels are either for pulling very heavy trains or in some cases for use on light rail that would be damaged if there were too much downward pressure from any particular wheel.

So much for the drivers; now for the leading truck wheels. If there is no leading truck the chances are 99 to 1 that the engine is used only for switching and is limited to speeds of 10 or 15 miles per hour. Ordinary HO engines can hardly run that slowly (1 foot in 4 to 6 seconds) unless you use special types of power pack with transistors and some kind of "pulse power."

If there are two leading truck wheels (one on each side), the engine is most likely a freight locomotive, and if the driving wheels are large its proper speed might be 45 miles per hour or occasionally higher.

Only engines with four guiding wheels, two on each side of the leading truck, are able to follow the rails at high speeds. Thus, practically all passenger trains and many fast freight trains are handled with such engines.

The trailing wheels may or may not be present in any of the cases mentioned so far. An engine without trailing wheels is most likely to be one built in the 1920's or even before. On the other hand, an engine with two trailing wheels would be larger and heavier and would be built since 1895 or more likely a little later, or into the 1930's. An engine with four trailing wheels would be still heavier and would be built since the mid-1920's.

In models the wheel arrangement has little to do with either speed or pulling power, but as we acquire more than one or two locomotives we tend to try to use them for the proper service according to the wheel arrangements.

In diesel and electric locomotives things are much simpler. Almost any but the smallest engine might be used for freight or passenger service. The smaller diesels are mostly switchers but many "road engines" might also be used for switching. The difference between the streamlined, curved-nose diesels and the narrow hood types is strictly a matter of looks. Un-

STEAM LOCOMOTIVE TYPE NAMES AND WHEEL ARRANGEMENTS

FRONT TRUCK	REAR TRUCK	COMMON USE	NUMBER OF DRIVING WHEELS			
			4	6	8	10
0	0	Switching	0-4-0 Four-wheel	0-6-0 Six-wheel	0-8-0 Eight-wheel	0-10-0 (Rare) Ten-wheel
2	0	General freight. Older engines, also for switching.	2-4-0 (Rare)	2-6-0 Mogul	2-8-0 Consolidation	2-10-0 Decapod
2	2	Heavier freight. Trailer truck supports larger firebox weight.	2-4-2 Columbia	2-6-2 Prairie	2-8-2 Mikado	2-10-2 Santa Fe
2	4	Modern freight. Still heavier firebox weight.			2-8-4 Berkshire	2-10-4 Texas
4	4	Fast freight and modern heavy passenger.	4-4-4 (Rare) Jubilee (Passenger)	4-6-4 Hudson (Passenger)	4-8-4 Northern	
4	2	Conventional for passenger service.	4-4-2 Atlantic	4-6-2 Pacific	4-8-2 Mountain	4-10-2 Southern Pacific
4	0	Older passenger and general use.	4-4-0 American	4-6-0 Ten-wheel	4-8-0 Twelve-wheel	4-10-0 Mastodon

der the skin the engines may be identical both in the model and on the real railroad. Most of the streamliners were built before 1950 and the narrow hood types were built since 1948. Since they are really alike, they can be mixed together on the same train if convenient for the company to do so.

If you are in doubt, the safest locomotive types to buy from the standpoint of simulating correct railroad practice will probably be the 2-8-2 (Mikado) for freight service, the 4-6-2 (Pacific) for passenger service, and the 0-6-0 (six-coupled) for switching;

or the hood-type diesel for any of these services. In the steam engines the numbers indicate the leading, driving, and trailing wheels counting *both* sides of the engine, not just the wheels you see at one time.

If your curves will be sharp, a Mogul (2-6-0) or Ten-Wheeler (4-6-0) would be better for freight, and the Ten-Wheeler and the Atlantic (4-4-2) would be well suited to passenger service. Actually these types are generally older and represent the days when railroads ran shorter trains and had sharper curves, just as on your model railroad.

All these types and more are available in HO size, and often are available as they appear or appeared on any of a number of different railroad companies. You can get many types of locomotives representing such well-known railroads as the Southern Pacific, the Pennsylvania, the Santa Fe, the Great Northern, the Baltimore & Ohio, etc. Some modelers like to specialize on one particular road.

In kit-assembled locomotives the variety is not as great, but you can get extra parts to change the detail. This is a source of a lot of fun but beyond the scope of this book.

11: Model locomotives

IN buying a good locomotive you want to consider the outward appearance, of course, but you also want to know what kind of a job the model can do and what to do if you have any trouble with it.

Here are the main things that make a difference between one model locomotive and another:

1. Performance.
2. Weight.
3. Amount of weight carried on powered wheels.
4. Kind of wheels.
5. Motor size and quality.
6. Gearing method and amount of gear reduction.
7. Method of electric pickup.
8. Radius of curves the engine can negotiate.
9. Availability of replacement parts.
10. Over-all construction and quality of materials.
11. Appearance.

A good average speed for model locomotives is about 1 foot per second, which is a scale 60 miles per hour. Many model locos, even switchers, are geared so they can go much faster than this. But a loco geared for lower speeds will run more smoothly when starting and going up and down hills, and its motor will not be nearly so likely to burn out with any load. After a little breaking in, a good engine will run unfalteringly at low as well as high speeds, providing its wheels and the track are clean and the electric contact to trucks or tender are not loose or oxidized.

Noise is often a consideration with geared locomotives, and it is very hard to correct. Noise comes from gears that don't mesh ideally either because

of the shape of the gears themselves or because they are adjusted too loosely or even too tightly. If you have seen other locomotives just like yours (same make and model) that are less noisy, you may want to send to the manufacturer for another set of gears and geared wheels, but this is no guarantee that they will be any better. Another more practical approach for an inexperienced modeler is to accept the gears as they are, but to put weight or material like sponge rubber inside the engine to dampen the noise. Molybdenum-type lubricants such as Molykote also help reduce noise. Fortunately, gear noises usually become less as gears wear in.

Getting pulling force in a model loco is often important, and it isn't accomplished by using a big motor as you might guess. The motor size has little to do with the maximum pull.

It's *weight* that has the most to do with pulling power. If the horizontal drag of a string of cars is more than ⅛ to ¼ the weight of the engine, the driving wheels will just slip and wear. One way to make an engine pull more cars is by adding more weight to it. A bigger motor without extra weight would only spin the wheels sooner and wear them out more quickly. If much of the engine's weight is on idle wheels, the pulling power is proportionately less. This is why those diesel and electric locos built with only one truck driving can pull only about half as many cars as those with both trucks driving.

The material the wheels are made of makes a difference too. Polished nickel-plated wheels slip more easily than brass or steel wheels. Some

plastic wheels are better than brass, others not as good. Some locomotives have rubberlike tires on some of the driving wheels, and these increase the pulling force by as much as 25 per cent over brass. They are often used to make up for the lack of driven wheels in the other truck.

Big motors are needed more to handle the heat than for their extra pulling power. If a locomotive has enough gear reduction, a small motor can pull the longest train very well. But the same locomotive geared for fast speeds will need a larger motor because more heat will be generated in its armature coil windings. Here are the principal things that can make a motor run hot:

1. Insufficient gear reduction, causing the motor to turn too slowly for the load.
2. Poor ventilation — only air can cool the motor.
3. Load too heavy.
4. Bearings or gears tight or in need of lubrication.
5. Motor too small, unable to dissipate heat.
6. Weak magnet, wasting energy in the motor.

A well-designed locomotive will have just enough weight to pull its proper load, but no excess weight. If you try to overload the engine the wheels merely slip, and this slippage automatically protects the motor from working harder and overheating.

If you have the opportunity to control an engine with a power pack equipped with an ammeter, you will notice that the ammeter shows a higher reading when the engine goes up a grade or when it has many cars to pull. The ammeter is a good indicator of load, and its reading doesn't ordinarily change very much with speed.

Most motors have an ampere rating of 0.6 a., and if the locomotive's weight is right the wheels will slip at about the time the load is increased enough to show a 0.6 a. reading on the meter. Some motors have lower or higher ratings. Many are listed in a chart in the book *How to Wire Your Model Railroad*.

To avoid damage, don't run a motor at a higher rating than its proper maximum for more than a minute or so. The more the overload, the less the time the motor can stand it before getting too hot.

Good motor magnets don't lose their magnetism in model railroad use. Weak magnets are very rare, but sometimes bargain-price motors have inferior magnets that look just like regular motor magnets yet cause overheating.

As I've already implied, a large gear reduction is good because it lowers the motor-heating current and at the same time it helps ventilation because the motor turns faster. It also allows for smoother control at low speeds. Engines with ordinary gearing usually stall at speeds of less than a scale 10 miles per hour. Good gearing runs more quietly; plastic gears also help.

Rubber-band drives

Rubber-band drives usually don't have enough speed reduction, but they partly make up for this by being very efficient. They do require quite a bit of maintenance (new bands, removal of hair from the belts, and so forth).

Athearn's rubber-band locos are the Model T's of HO railroading. You can get many accessories for them and you can get a Hobbytown chassis and gear drive to fit them or a Pittman motor and gear reduction unit. Many train sets other than Athearn's come with this same loco. In some cases the Athearn plastic shell is used over a different make of mechanism. There are also Athearn locos with gears instead of bands. If they run smoothly they are to be preferred.

Locomotive wiring

An HO locomotive should go in the same direction as all your other HO locos when you put it on the track. If it goes in the opposite direction, there's a flaw in its wiring. Sometimes it's because the magnet was turned the wrong way around when the motor was assembled, but you don't have to turn it back again to correct this. Let's consider a correctly

wired loco. See Figs. 11-1 and 11-2.

Whether it's a steam or diesel type, current is picked up from the rails at one side and passed to the brushes of the motor. The second motor brush is grounded to the motor frame in most cases, and through the frame it is connected without wires to the wheels on the other side of the engine.

Ideally, all wheels on each side of a loco should have electrical pickup arrangements so all wheels on each rail make useful electrical contact. This is the case on a few locomotives but more often the forward wheels on the right side and the rear wheels on the left are used for electrical pickup. The remaining wheels are then completely insulated and neutral. On close examination you may find these neutral wheels insulated either by being of plastic or by having a plastic bushing near their hub or rim. In a few instances axles are made in halves and pushed into plastic collars or drums located between the wheels. In the rubber-band engines these insulating drums also serve as pulleys for the drive mechanism.

When you think of right and left in a locomotive, consider it from the viewpoint of the men who would be sitting in the cab facing forward. If you turn the engine over, don't forget that, depending on how you turn it over, right and left can all too easily get reversed.

A loco should move forward when the right-hand rail is connected to positive on the power pack. If you don't know which is positive, you can make a comparison with the operation of other locomotives.

If the loco goes the wrong way, you can correct it. If it's a rubber-band drive, twist the bands the other way around at the point where they make a half turn. With some locos you can turn both trucks halfway around so that the pickup wheels are on opposite rails. Or you can take the trucks apart and turn all the axles end for end.

But usually the easiest way is to interchange the two wires to the two motor brushes. Often one brush is grounded, but by bending a lug upward, you can unground this brush and connect the motor wire to it. Then ground the other brush.

The normal wiring for a steam loco is with the insulated drivers on the left. Thus, the right wheels and the loco frame are connected to the grounded motor brush. The wire from the other brush is connected to the tender frame and via the frame to the wheels under the tender's left side. The tender's right-side wheels are insulated.

The brush connection to the tender frame is done in two ways. On most American-made locomotives there is a wire direct from brush to a plug or screw in the tender. A fiber drawbar couples the engine so it can pull the tender without metallic connection. This is because any metal contact from engine frame to tender frame would cause a short circuit, since each is grounded to a different rail.

Other locomotives often have a metal drawbar between engine and tender but the engine end of it is insulated from the engine frame. In these engines the wire from the mo-

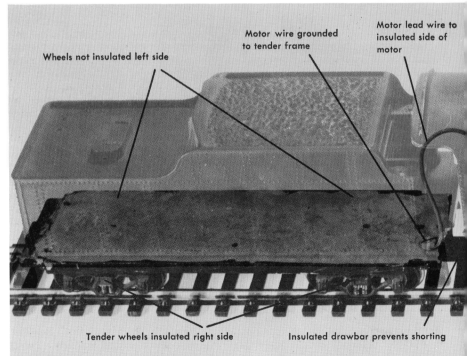

Motor wire grounded to tender frame

Motor lead wire to insulated side of motor

Wheels not insulated left side

Tender wheels insulated right side

Insulated drawbar prevents shorting

Fig. 11-1. Typical steam-type locomotive wiring and motor arrangement.

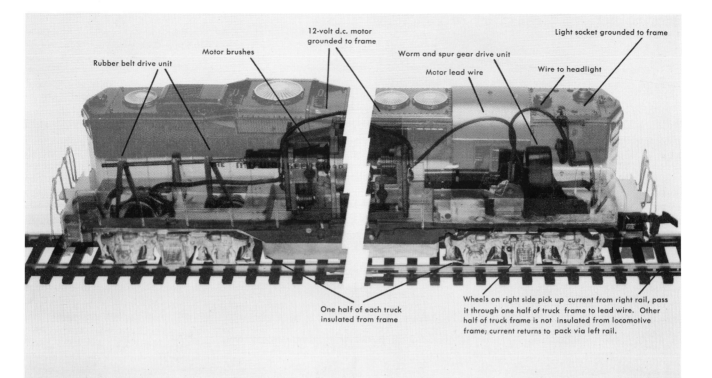

12-volt d.c. motor grounded to frame

Worm and spur gear drive unit

Light socket grounded to frame

Motor brushes

Motor lead wire

Wire to headlight

Rubber belt drive unit

One half of each truck insulated from frame

Wheels on right side pick up current from right rail, pass it through one half of truck frame to lead wire. Other half of truck frame is not insulated from locomotive frame; current returns to pack via left rail.

Fig. 11-2. Composite of two types of diesel-type locomotives. The left half shows rubber-band drive; the right half, one of several types of gear drive. Actually the **two types of drive would never be found in the same engine; each end of engine would have same kind of drive. Halves of two different types of motors are at center.**

tor's hot brush goes to the screw that holds the front end of this bar and thus makes connection through the bar to the tender frame and left rear wheels.

Metal vs. plastic

Since weight is desirable, a locomotive with an all-metal body, especially if it is thick metal, will pull more

cars than a plastic-shelled locomotive of the same size. Also, metal is tougher and handrails and other metal details will withstand a good bit more handling than plastic.

In other ways, plastic is more practical. It usually can be replaced at low cost. It absorbs more shock if a loco falls to the floor. It is easier to paint if you use a spray gun and re-

pairs and changes in detail are often easier to make. If you are interested in kits, a plastic body is much easier to clean up than a die-cast one. Plastic has the fault of being easily marred by spilled cement or thinner, and in some cases it warps out of shape. A plastic engine or one made of thin metal can also be a sounding board for noisy gearing or bearings.

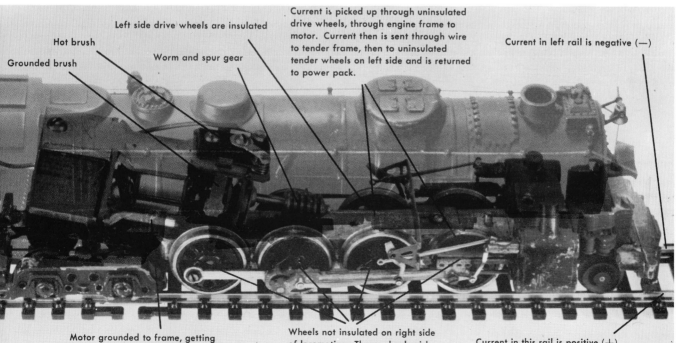

Left side drive wheels are insulated

Current is picked up through uninsulated drive wheels, through engine frame to motor. Current then is sent through wire to tender frame, then to uninsulated tender wheels on left side and is returned to power pack.

Hot brush

Grounded brush

Worm and spur gear

Current in left rail is negative (—)

Motor grounded to frame, getting current through uninsulated drivers

Wheels not insulated on right side of locomotive. These wheels pick up current from right rail.

Current in this rail is positive (+)

How to get top locomotive performance

Experts rebuild parts of the mechanisms of their locomotives to reduce friction, particularly at motor or worm gear thrust bearings, and to make sure every part fits perfectly. But there is a lot you can do with simple tools to keep your ready-to-run locomotives in good running order.

In general, you want to do these things:

1. Keep friction to a minimum.
2. Make sure parts have freedom to move as they should.
3. Insure that enough spring tension or weight holds idle wheels as well as running wheels on the track, but otherwise with as much of the weight as possible still supported on the running wheels.
4. Make sure that parts that should be insulated from one another don't accidentally touch.

If you take these things as the basis for systematic trouble-hunting, you can find 99 per cent of the troubles you'll have with a locomotive or car.

Add light model oil or clock oil to motor wicks and to the axle bearings of all idle wheels on locos, tenders and cars. Use a hypo-type oiler so the oil enters the bearing but doesn't get all over the wheels or truck frame. Too much oil attracts more dirt.

For gears and driving axles use a model or fishing reel grease like Lubriplate or Molykote, etc. Use it sparingly at axles, but you may lather the gears. If gears are in a case, use plenty of grease inside.

General maintenance

A new locomotive has not necessarily been lubricated, so it should be checked right away, checked again in about a week, and then every few weeks if it is run frequently. If run only occasionally, check about once a year, and look for grease that has hardened inside gear cases.

You can remove the body, if necessary, by spreading the center of most plastic-body locos slightly, like opening a cracked egg. Other locos have screws that hold the body shell in place, often extending down from the roof to a point under the floor.

Steam-type loco bodies are held with one screw at the front and various arrangements at the rear. The front screw may be down the stack or else directly below the stack on the underside of the frame. At the rear there may be screws underneath on each side, a center screw, or in the case of small Mantua locos, no rear screws at all.

When removing a steam boiler, take care not to bend the front railing wires as they pull out of holes in the pilot (cowcatcher). You may also have to work carefully to get the firebox around the motor.

In any case, don't loosen screws you are not sure about without analyzing them first. They may loosen important assemblies or adjustments.

If locomotive gears show an accumulation of worn metal, grit, fiber or hair, or if they're completely dry, wash them before you relubricate. Apply ordinary cleaning fluid or other grease solvents with a watercolor brush and catch the drippings in a dish. Do this in a well-ventilated room. After rinsing out the dirt and old oil, let the parts dry out before relubricating.

When you lubricate, look for loosening screws and sagging couplers. You may save damage by finding these before they cause trouble. The screws that hold side rods and valve parts on steam locomotives can be particularly troublesome.

Gear adjustment

Most gears are fixed in the proper place at the factory, but sometimes worm gears need adjusting if mounted directly on the motor shaft. You'll usually find one or two screws on the underside of the motor which loosen the motor and its shaft so the motor can rock or slide and thus adjust the gear mesh spacing.

Gears should mesh so deeply that each tooth almost, but not quite, touches the mating tooth behind it as well as the tooth in front. If the mesh is so deep a tooth touches two other teeth at the same time, friction called gear bind occurs, the motor will run hotter, and the gears will wear faster.

On the other hand, too loose a gear mesh can also cause gear wear and also excessive bucking of a train running downhill, as will be explained in a moment. In severe cases of loose mesh gears may even buzz past each each other, or lose a step every once in a while.

If you can adjust the gear spacing while the motor is running, increase the mesh until you notice it is beginning to reduce the motor speed, then back away just enough so motor and gears run freely. If you can't make this running test, you can use a film of thin wax paper as a spacer between gears while you tighten the adjustment screws. Remove the torn bits of paper; if the adjustment was made carefully the motor should now turn easily.

Adjustment for other types of gears is done the same way in principle. Sometimes slips of thin paper can be used to spread the parts which hold the shafts of gears that are too tightly meshed. Likewise, a little metal can be filed away from the shaft support if you suspect gears are too far apart.

Gear noise can sometimes be reduced by using molybdenum disulphide grease such as Molykote.

Uneven motor speed when the engine is run on its back indicates either a bent motor shaft, gears with their pivot hole off center, gears with poor shape, or in the case of a steam-type loco, side or valve rods binding. Don't attempt to correct any of these things until you've had a little experience with tools and modelmaking. Usually, good replacement parts will be the inexpensive way out.

Derailments

Many derailments are caused by parts that do not allow wheels to swing far enough to the side. On Athearn locos the truck frames sometimes not only short-circuit on the sides of the coupler housing (Fig. 11-4), but they are also prevented from turning far enough and so derail at any kink in the track or any bad rail joint. Clipping or filing off material from an offending part is the usual solution.

Often it takes careful study to determine just where parts rub. If you run an engine very slowly with pulse power you can stop the operation at the point where derailment occurs to study it.

Diesels and other two-truck locos, as well as all cars, will derail easily if their trucks are too rigid. Trucks must be able to tilt to either side and rock forward and back freely, enough so you could lift any adjacent two wheels at least $\frac{1}{32}$" from the rails with all other car or loco wheels still on the track.

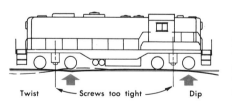

Twist — Screws too tight → Dip

Fig. 11-3. Truck-mounted locomotives (and, for that matter, cars) must be so pivoted that the trucks can not only turn on curves but also nod on dips and rock on track twisted out of level. With some engines pivot screws and sideframe screws have to be loosened or washers placed between truck and frame to accomplish this. Be sure that any truck that is supposed to be insulated remains insulated by using a fiber instead of a metal washer.

Fig. 11-4. Trouble spots that cause derailments and "shorts." See text.

The motor wire can be a source of mechanical trouble. If it is too short it can lift wheels from the rails or prevent a truck from turning to the side far enough to negotiate curves. If your loco operates all right until the body shell is put on, the shell may be pressing on this wire. The wire can also get pinched alongside the motor and bind the shell or prevent the motor or gears from turning.

Loud buzzing, short circuits or a dead motor may occur when the body shell is put on if the motor is not properly centered in its space and seated on the frame. The body shell then touches the motor or motor wire, or interferes with the normal spring action of the brushes. On some locos, anything pulling on the motor wire will also interfere with brush springing. Uneven tension of the bands in a rubber-band-drive engine can lift wheels from the rails at the slightest provocation.

Bucking and stalling

Some locomotives buck when starting or running downhill. This happens at the point where the engine begins to coast. At this moment all the play in the gears and the worm shaft is loosened and the motor speeds ahead for a moment. Meanwhile the cars and the weight of the engine itself tend to want to go still faster down the hill. As soon as they overtake the more nearly constant speed of the gearing, the gears get loaded on the opposite side of their teeth from normal. This slows the motor, and the momentum of the body and cars presses all the harder against the gears, all but stopping the engine. The remedy is to reduce the lost motion in the gears as already explained, to use a better gear lubricant, or to use an elaborate type of transistor throt-

tle which can entirely eliminate this type of bucking.

A sort of bucking also can be caused by momentary interruptions of electric power, either from short circuits or poor connections. This is very common with the connections to and in the tender of steam locomotives. Any electrical cause of bucking will probably become a complete stall if you run the engine very slowly.

Short-circuit stalling occurs when parts that should be electrically isolated from each other accidentally touch. The flanges of center wheels on long locos may touch hot rails in a switch. Pilots may touch wires or other metal parts near the track or on adjacent cars, or they may dip so low as to touch the rails. On sharp curves, a tender body may touch its corner to the locomotive, or metal diesels and any metal cars may touch corners, causing short circuits if the cars are grounded to opposite rails. Long drawbar links or couplers will prevent this. It is a good idea to have cars insulated completely from both rails. Many new cars are built this way.

Metal couplers should also be insulated. When they aren't, a short can develop through a coupler from one grounded frame to another.

If a car truck gets turned halfway around, it causes a short circuit through the metal frame, particularly troublesome on steam loco tenders. Also, if you take wheels out of a truck and happen to replace them backwards, they cause a short circuit. Look carefully and you'll see that the insulated wheel has a plastic bushing, plastic layer near the rim, or baked varnish coating on the axle.

A most common cause of short circuits even in manufactured equipment is when some "hot" part of a truck touches part of a grounded frame. In Fig. 11-4 the brake hanger of the Athearn GP-9 truck had been touching the side of the coupler housing on sharp curves. This caused short circuits that made the black spots above the pencil point. In operation the engine bucked. It stalled only if run very slowly. The truck frame on the other side didn't cause short circuits, for it wasn't hot, but it did press hard enough to prevent the truck wheels from following 18″ radius curves. So both sides of the truck frame had to be filed away at the point indicated by the pencil.

Short-circuit stalling is indicated by a general dimming of any lights powered from the same pack.

Stalling also occurs from broken or open circuits (lights become brighter). This can be caused by dirty track or by something lifting the wheels from the rails, like deep flanges. Sometimes

a wire gets broken inside its insulation where the break may not be suspected. Poorly soldered joints may also have a hidden break. A loose rail joiner or connecting screw or spring also causes broken electrical circuits.

Locked wheels

When wheels won't turn, look for dirt in gears, motor wire caught in gears, some body part touching wheels, gears or rods. Also, look for a screw missing from side rods, a driving wheel loose on its axle, or misfitted valve gear parts. Sometimes a motor commutator plate gets loose or the motor shaft is bent or just too tight against the worm gear. In a few locos the axle bearings are in halves and may be clamped too tight. A motor brush may be worn or cracked and lodged at an angle that prevents the commutator from turning. A broken brush can also cause stalling or excessive sparking.

A broken wire in the motor armature windings will make the motor stall at one point, but it will run if you start it with your fingers.

Sluggish running

Steady but generally sluggish running occurs from a bad case of oxide on wheels or rails as often as from any other cause. (See page 12.) Or, if you accidentally leave the pack set for pulse power, you will wonder why engines won't reach top speeds. Some may not even start.

Iron filings attracted to the motor in the space between the armature and field magnet can drag on the armature or even lock it. Clean out what you can with paper, tweezers, etc.; then run the motor fast so centrifugal force will throw many of the filings away. Then recheck the cleaning.

If the twist of one or two of the rubber bands of a rubber-band drive are reversed, the engine will either stall or run sluggishly. A missing or loose band can have the same effect. Hair can also catch a band to retard its turning. The two bands to a single truck should be equally tight.

Excessive friction in the locomotive is a dangerous cause of sluggish running, as it can overheat the motor, so watch for this one. Anything that makes the motor turn harder makes the motor run warmer.

Motor adjustment

I've already mentioned that some troubles occur from misshapen motor brushes and weakened springs. Sometimes you can improve the operation of a motor by slightly changing the spring tension on the brushes. This is a desirable adjustment. Try for the fastest speed at a given power pack setting. Excessive sparking isn't good but a small even line of sparks is common. Bad sparking comes from unevenness of the commutator surface, eroded gaps between the commutator plates, loose or misshapen brushes, or weak springs. Slight commutator unevenness can be polished off by holding a very fine abrasive cloth or stick against the commutator while the motor is turning by itself. Don't use anything that will scratch a penny.

Spare brushes are sold by better-equipped shops. Get the right size for the motor and replace brushes before they are worn shorter than about ⅛".

Will too many volts hurt a motor?

Not ordinarily. Excess volts make a motor run faster, but good motors can run on 24 v. or more without *electrical* damage. On the other hand, if the motor has a *mechanical* defect, speed may damage it. A loose commutator plate may fly off. An uneven commutator will make the brushes bounce.

Motors are more likely to be damaged by heat when overloaded. The more load and friction a motor has to overcome, the more amperes of current it draws automatically from the power pack (regardless of voltage). Amperes produce some heat in all wiring, but produce much more in small wire such as that in the motor. Thus the more work a motor has to do, the hotter it gets. The critical point is when the motor is so hot that plastic parts are melted or split, or when insulation burns off the wire or soldered joints come apart. This point is well above a sizzling temperature and with a little observation you can avoid motor burnouts. Average-size motors will stay safely cool when drawing any amount up to 0.6 ampere. (A few motors have other ratings, but the principle is the same.) If you make the motor pull a heavier load, it draws more current, and if it draws 0.9 ampere it will develop heat more than twice as fast as normal. So an overload can be critical. The best precaution with a motor is to check the loco with its load, using an ammeter. You can do this occasionally, or you can install a meter permanently on your control panel.

Running a hot motor slowly doesn't help it cool off if the load is still the same. Take off cars instead and run at any speed.

After you first start an engine, its performance may improve as the lubricant is warmed and distributed. Later the loco may slow down again. This is particularly common with some motors in Athearn's rubber-band locos and it is because the motor gets so warm that the windings actually have increased electrical resistance. This tends to make them still warmer and at the same time requires more voltage to get the same speed. No harm is done if you watch that the motor doesn't get so hot that its wires will burn their insulation.

12: Cars

IF you think there are a lot of different locomotives in HO, wait till you hear about cars! There must be more than 1000 different cars available; most come in kit form, but many come ready to run. Recently, I counted more than 250 boxcars alone, including the different lettering schemes available on each make of car. And if you count all the ways you can add decals to plain-painted cars, there's hardly any limit at all.

Various makes of cars are just about equal in performance, so you can buy largely for variety and looks.

Freight trains are made up of the cars that represent the areas they serve. If you're in a mining area, you'll see mostly gondola and hopper cars or little ore cars, with empties going toward the mine and full cars coming back. In a fruit-growing area or near a meat-packing plant, refrigerator cars prevail.

Stock cars will be seen around packing plants and also in cattle regions. A stock train often has a "drovers' car." This is either a special passenger car or a caboose with extra windows so the men who care for the critters can ride along with the train. Special double-deck cars are used for sheep and hogs, and cars with screen wire are for poultry. All these are made in HO, even though your hobby shop may not always have them in stock.

Heavy machinery calls for flatcars or even special cars with extra trucks to carry additional weight, or drop-center cars to carry high loads.

Tank cars are used for petroleum and acids; wooden tanks for pickles.

One of the most versatile cars of today is the covered hopper car. This is like the coal hopper, but it has a closed top with loading hatches. The cover keeps materials like cement, grain, quicklime or dehydrated chemicals from getting wet or dirty.

Most freight trains on real railroads have far more boxcars than any other type. Boxcars carry just about everything the other cars carry at times, but their construction is most suited to goods in crates or containers. If you want a realistic-looking train, go heavy on the boxcars and include one or two of the long 50-footers.

In the last few years the piggyback car has suddenly appeared in quantity in American trains. Only a few varieties are now available in models but the number will probably increase. The standard truck semitrailer mounted on a standard railroad flatcar is so high that it cannot pass through some railroad tunnels or under bridges. For this reason there are special flatcars that let the semitrailer sit in a well in the car floor. There are also special low trailers that can get through tight places. Besides these methods of meeting clearance restrictions, many railroads have been lowering the tracks in tunnels and under bridges to get greater clearance for the piggybacks.

Another recent trend that we may see more of is the use of freight cars up to 85 feet long, the same length as

A busy executive with only a couple of evenings a week and an occasional weekend to spend at the work table can build an amazing amount of model equipment from kits in 2 or 3 years. What you see here is the work of one such executive. The view also represents a small part of the great variety of car and locomotive kits available in HO.

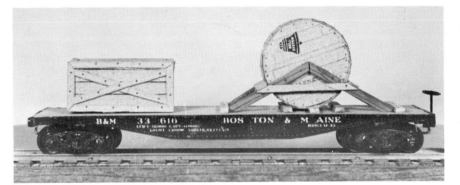

the longest passenger cars. These won't be of much use to the fellow with very sharp curves on his pike.

As you buy cars, go heavy on the boxcars that are just plain boxcar red (in various shades) and you'll find the train will look more realistic than a train made up mostly of wild colors. Cars that have been "weathered" or "aged" also make the train more realistic.

Passenger cars

Passenger cars aren't as popular as freight cars in HO. This is partly because they offer less variety and aren't quite so colorful as freight cars, and partly because they don't offer as many opportunities for switching. Also, their length makes them a little awkward in yards and on curves.

The longest prototype railroad cars scale to as much as 12" long in HO, and these cars are not well suited to curves of less than 30" radius. For this reason, most HO cars are either abbreviated versions of long cars or else modeled from shorter originals. In our scenic settings, these shorter cars usually look long enough as they are. A 60-foot car can be run on most model railroads and will make it around an 18" radius curve (with some amazing overhang).

On a typical passenger train, the mail, express, and baggage cars are placed directly behind the locomotive. Sometimes there are also one or more "express refrigerator" cars equipped with steam hoses and other passenger fittings so they can handle milk and other food quickly. Behind all these cars come the cars with plain seats, the coaches. Then comes the diner, but it may be switched out of the train at certain hours. Somewhere behind the diner there may be a parlor car for de luxe day travel at extra cost. Also behind the diner are all types of sleeping cars, the last one with a club and observation section.

Sometimes "combine" cars are used. The most common is a combination mail, baggage, and perhaps express, all in one car. Often, one of these facilities is combined with the first coach. A diner may be combined with a parlor car if both can be small.

The older sleeping cars have upper and lower berths and sometimes private bedrooms or compartments at one end. Modern sleepers are all of the bedroom, compartment or roomette type, or a combination. Roomettes are very small bedrooms on each side of a center aisle. All other modern compartment sleepers have a corridor down one side. Duplex roomette cars have half the roomettes in raised position so the windows are staggered up and down along the side of the car.

These flatcars were built from kits by a war veteran at Lawson General Hospital in Atlanta, Ga. He built various loads so the one type of car produced a lot of variety. Part of the fun in this kind of creative extension of kit building lies in digging up the information on how cars should be loaded. Maj. M. M. Kissane took the photos but did not give the patient's name.

What is the NMRA?

Ever since it was formed in 1936, the National Model Railroad Association has been a guiding light of our hobby. It has some 26,000 members, including most of the more active model railroaders. Every model railroader is invited to become a member. The dues are modest, and include a subscription to the organization's monthly newsletter, the *Bulletin*. To join the NMRA, write to P. O. Box 2186, Indianapolis, IN 46206.

The NMRA is responsible for uniform wheel standards among most manufacturers of HO equipment, and it is a tribute to the NMRA that its standards and recommendations work well.

The organization holds annual local and national conventions, issues interesting and useful data sheets on the engineering and operating phases of the hobby, and generally sponsors creative development as well as fellowship in model railroading.

Dome cars can be of any passenger-carrying type — diner, sleeper, coach, and so forth. They look very nice in a model train, especially if they're softly lighted at night.

Model cars and rolling quality

Almost any HO car will give good service, and if something isn't right, it's usually easy to fix. And cars are so easy to assemble from kits that you needn't consider only the ready-to-run cars.

Good detail and easy assembly have made plastic cars and kits very popular in HO, but even with their built-in weights most plastic cars are not heavy enough for good operation. They derail if used near the front of any but short trains, and they derail when backing or uncoupling. For good operation, all cars should weigh about ½ ounce for each inch of their length (or a trifle less with very good track and easy-rolling trucks; likewise a little more if the car does not have such good trucks). You can add fish sinkers or type metal, or fashion a load from wood or plaster, or you can pour Cerrobend* into cavities in the car. Cerrobend is handy for increasing the pull of locomotives, too, by adding weight in any body cavities.

---

*Cerrobend is the trademark name for an expensive bismuth alloy sold through distributors of the Cerro de Pasco Company and at some hobby shops. It weighs about the same as lead, but will melt below the boiling point of water and thus can be poured into wood or plastic cars and locomotive bodies without damage. Write the company at 300 Park Avenue, New York 22, N. Y., for literature on model railroad uses and for address of nearest distributor.

As with locomotives, car trucks must be able to rock to each side and a little fore and aft as well. As car troubles are all covered in either the locomotive or coupler chapters, they will not be repeated here.

Wheels that roll freely allow you to run longer trains, but more important is the fact that free-rolling wheels cut derailments in half.

While many modelers get along with poor-rolling trucks, those who have taken the trouble to replace the culls with good wheels or whole trucks have been satisfied that it was worth the cost of replacement.

Arrange a 36" length of straight track on a board so one end of the track is 1" higher than the other. Then lubricate the trucks on your cars, Fig. 12-1, and try rolling them on this hill. Some may take a slight nudge to start, but if any car won't pick up speed it is a candidate for better wheels or trucks. You aren't out much because most sets of poor wheels came with cars that were not too expensive in the first place.

You can get sets of wheels with RP25 contour mounted on Torrington-made needle-bearing axles which will fit into many makes of trucks, or you can buy several makes of new trucks with these wheels or equivalent included. Torrington axles running in Delrin plastic bearings are particularly free-rolling. Some kinds of plastic wheels are not good at all.

Many experts prefer metal wheels. These wheels have the advantage of not collecting as much gummy dirt as plastic wheels when rolling over the track. On the other hand, some plastic wheels give excellent performance.

Some makes of trucks, especially the ones used in train sets for the toy as well as the serious HO market, have couplers mounted on an arm extending from the truck. This looks like a good idea because it keeps the coupler nearer the center of the track. Such couplers are all right on long passenger cars but they often cause a great deal of trouble on freight cars when they are pushed during switching maneuvers. Then the slightest imperfection in the track can cause a derailment.

If you have such trouble, you can either use different trucks or you can make a file mark and break the coupler arm off the truck. Then you can buy another coupler with a mounting box called a "draft gear" and install it with small screws or pins under the end of the car body.

Wheels out of gauge

Many cars are made with wheels pushed onto axles. If the "back-to-back" distance isn't right they will derail (Fig. 2-6). It's a good idea to get a National Model Railroad Association wheel and track gauge and use it to check the wheels on a car or locomotive that frequently derails. You may find some wheels spread too far apart or too close together. They will still hold the rails most of the time, but they'll derail at the least track imperfection. Warning: Study carefully the instructions that come with the gauge!

Usually you can twist out-of-gauge wheels into position on their metal axles. One-piece wheel and axle pairs are usually in gauge, but if they are not they should be replaced.

Fig. 12-1. Here is an easy way to make certain a tiny droplet of oil makes its way to the end of the axle. Note how fingers pushing down on diagonally opposite wheels automatically raise remaining wheels for more convenient oiling. Excessive oil on a model spells trouble both in dirt collection at the axle and in poor traction from leakage onto the rails. The oiler shown is a tube type available at hobby shops. Use only light clock or model oil.

The Tiny Line is a testimonial to the therapeutic value of the hobby of model railroading. The pike was built by patients of Atascadero State Hospital in California. The project was started on a Ping-pong table; when membership tripled the railroad was expanded to cover a 6 x 18-foot space. A lot of the track and parts of the railroad, and many of the buildings, were donated by members of model railroad clubs in nearby communities.

A Lackawanna diesel heads a long freight over an unfinished ravine on Jim Frye's Cobwebs, Dust & Ashes RR.

Jim used real rock slabs and chips in modeling the ravine. The rock will later be blended in with plaster.

Along the right of way

E. L. Moore's Elizabeth Valley RR. is a good example of putting lots of interest into a small space. The EV is only 4 x 6 feet, but the pond, shrubbery, mountainous terrain and painted backdrop make it seem much larger.

Werner Gubitz of Palm Desert, Calif., took a tip from the prototype railroads when he started building equipment for his pike. He logically figured that the prototype often designs certain equipment to suit conditions on the road. So he did the same for his Weeville Western; he cut a Varney Aerotrain apart to build this fancy powered car. Using your imagination is part of the fun of model railroading — "imagineering," some call it.

13: Couplers

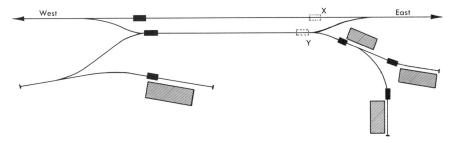

Fig. 13-1. Place ramps on main line for parting the train and on spurs at proper locations for spotting cars. Eastbound trains need ramps at X and Y.

PART of the fun of HO railroading comes from switching cars and entire trains, and here the couplers are the star performers. You can make HO cars couple together anywhere just by backing one car into another. When the cars pull ahead they remain coupled.

Uncoupling is done without the need of wires or other special gadgets except for an "uncoupling ramp" which is laid between the rails. Since uncoupling is desired only at certain places, most fellows buy enough ramps so one can be left at each location.

To uncouple a cut of cars on a side track, you push the cars until the couplers you wish to open are directly over the ramp. Then you reverse the engine and pull. The couplers that are over the ramp uncouple and your cut of cars is left behind. To couple again, you push the cars a little farther so the couplers are not above the ramp; then when you pull, the couplers remain coupled.

Every siding where you'd like to leave cars standing should have a ramp at the place where you want to uncouple. There should be another ramp on the main track nearby (Fig. 13-1) so you can break a train at any point between engine and caboose to pick up or set out a car at the side track.

There are several types of couplers in use in HO railroading. At first you will naturally use the couplers that come with train sets and some kits. These are the mechanical horn-hook type. They were once known as the "X2F" and also as the "NMRA" type, but both names are incorrect.

You have to know a bit of history to understand why I will both praise and condemn these horn-hook mechanical couplers. Paul Mallery invented them in the fifties at just the time when HO train sets were a new idea. He let anyone use them, so rather than favor any existing coupler maker, the many train set manufacturers adopted versions of the new horn-hook. This universal acceptance was far better than had happened earlier in the larger toy sizes and still occurs in Europe, where each manufacturer has his own coupler. It helped make HO train sets very popular.

On the other hand, it was also its own undoing. Each maker had slight variations in his couplers; none followed Mallery's specifications exactly. The result was tragic. Some couplers would not work well with others. Most were not mounted properly, for little study was given to this part of the problem. Worse yet, no one has devised an uncoupling ramp that is dependable with all makes of horn-hook mechanical coupler.

You will not get good performance with your horn-hooks unless you make sure they meet these requirements:

● They must be mounted at the proper height.

● They must not sag nor rise from this height when passing through ramps and over switches and crossings.

● They must not twist in their sockets.

● They must swing the right

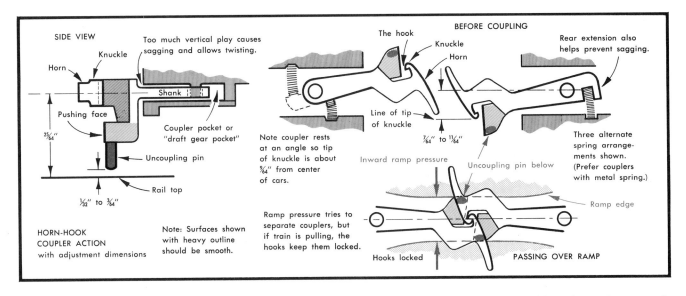

Fig. 13-2. When installing horn-hook couplers on your cars, check the vertical measurements of pin height above railhead and the height of the coupler centerline frequently. If the pin is not adjusted correctly, it may catch on switch frogs and cause derailments, or it may not go through the ramps properly. If couplers sag, do not shorten their pins but use shims to return them to operating height. In order for the couplers to uncouple, train must be backed slightly to gain slack in the couplers, allowing the two knuckles to swing to the side.

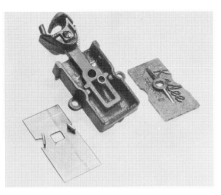

Fig. 13-3. Top, left: Kadee Magne-Matic MK-4 and MKD-4 coupler assembled in its draft-gear box. Adapter plate at left, cover at right. Top, center: Kadee Magne-Matic MK-9 and MKD-9. This type of coupler is designed for use on truck-mounted installations. Top, right: Kadee Magne-Matic MK-6 and MKD-6 assembled in the special draft-gear box which comes with the coupler. Long shank allows wide coupler swing. Directly right: Rail Line magnetic coupler assembled in its draft-gear box. L-shaped pin operates this coupler. Far right: Kadee RA Magne-Action coupler assembled in draft-gear box.

amount to the side — no more, no less.

● They must freely swing to couple with a mate when cars come together.

● The hook within the hook (see Fig. 13-2) must prevent uncoupling in a ramp when cars are pulled through.

● But the hooks should release if cars are slackened while in the ramp.

● Ramp side pressures should not derail cars.

In practice this means that you should go over all your cars and engines and check couplers for looseness, improper height, rough action when swung to side, and so on. Since this means a bit of work, many model railroaders prefer to replace the couplers entirely with one of the magnetic types. These overcome most of the objections and are generally easier to maintain.

Horn-hook magnetics

There are two general types of magnetic couplers. One is the horn-hook, which will mate with the mechanical horn-hook. This is a big advantage during your changeover period. The other is the knuckle-type magnetic coupler made by Kadee. This has unique advantages of its own, but let's discuss the horn-hook first.

When the mechanical horn-hook is pulled through a ramp, the two springy sides of the ramp (pink channel in Fig. 13-2) try to squeeze the uncoupling pins toward each other. But they don't succeed in unhooking the couplers unless there is slack in

the train. When the train is pulling, the hook within the main hook prevents the release.

The magnetic horn-hooks work the same way except that the ramp is a flat bar magnet between the rails. Instead of engaging a pin, it attracts the magnetic couplers in such a way that they open unless not in slack.

There are two fine makes of magnetic horn-hook coupler: the Rail Line Magnetic and the Magne-Action. (The Magne-Action is actually made by

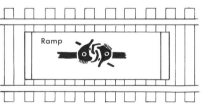

Normal coupled position — cars being pulled over ramp.

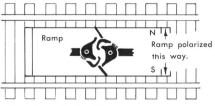

Slack bunched — knuckles open.

Fig. 13-4. The Kadee magnetic ramp is polarized crosswise so couplers' "air hoses" spread and open knuckles if cars slacken while over magnet.

Kadee — but do not confuse it with "Kadee couplers," for that term usually refers to the knuckle type that is also made by Kadee.)

The Rail Line Magnetic and the Magne-Action use different sorts of ramps, but they will mate with each other and also with mechanical horn-hooks. With either type you will get good performance, because the mounting design is good and because all your couplers will be alike.

The Rail Line Magnetic will also uncouple over a Kadee magnetic ramp, but the Magne-Action has a special ramp all its own. On the other hand, the Magne-Action has the advantage of coming in a number of mounting styles, making it easier to fit to some cars and engines.

Delayed action; electric ramps

At this point I should mention delayed action. You already know that it takes slack motion, either pausing or backing, to uncouple cars over a ramp. However, most couplers of the magnetic type also feature delayed action. This means that once uncoupled over a ramp, you can then push a car farther down the line to leave it anywhere you wish. Thus, with one ramp at the entrance track to a yard you could spot cars on any track at any distance. The old way, you had to have a ramp at each place you wanted to leave a car.

Delayed action is accomplished by preventing couplers from re-engaging on the ramp, once uncoupled. They do

Fig. 13-5. Marco coupler uses a solenoid ramp to attract unlocking pin downward. Spring then opens knuckle in a manner similar to a real coupler.

Fig. 13-6. The Roundhouse coupler, shown at the left, has the same working scheme as a real railroad coupler. The dummy coupler at right has no moving parts; it is often used because of its small size. No fully automatic coupler is quite as small, but dummy can mate with a Kadee if filed slightly.

not re-engage until again slackened after pushing them beyond the ramp. You can understand this a lot easier by seeing it done than by reading about it in a book.

Sometimes delayed action is a nuisance because it takes two more moves to get a car uncoupled and then re-coupled than it takes without delayed action. When you don't want delayed action you can use an electric-coil ramp such as Kadee sells. This will work the Rail Line Magnetic and the Kadee Magne-Matic, but not the Magne-Action coupler. The electric-coil ramp is also preferable in any mainline track: using ordinary magnetic ramps, accidental slack will break a train when you don't want it broken. The electric-coil ramp is magnetized for uncoupling only when you push a button. I connect mine with switch machine coils so that both work from the same button. (This idea is illustrated in the book *How to Wire Your Model Railroad.*) An electric ramp is more difficult to install but is well worth the trouble in mainline locations.

Knuckle magnetics

The Kadee Magne-Matic coupler looks much like a real railroad coupler, and it has the advantage of being at center position when uncoupled, rather than at the side. It has gained great respect among model railroaders since the late fifties and early sixties, when some major improvements were made. The coupler can be mounted in two ways, for delayed action or not, as you prefer. It's all a matter of slightly different side pressure, and the same parts are used in both types except that ramps of different widths are used.

Besides appearance, the Kadee line has the advantage of having a number of different mounting types, making it very easy to adapt the coupler to almost every car and loco made.

The MKD-5 coupler should be used in most cases, as it is easy to install either in the pocket (box) supplied or directly in the car's own pocket.

Other types are made for installing on long cars (MKD-6) and locomotives (various styles). Kadee instruc-

tions recommend which type to use.

To decide for yourself whether to use the couplers you now have, or magnetics of the horn-hook or of the knuckle type, I would recommend that you visit home or club railroads where each type is in use. The owners will tell you all the advantages of each, and maybe you can learn the faults as well by a little discerning questioning. I'm using Kadees, but I must admit I've seen fine operation with all the others.

Marco couplers

The Marco is another magnetically operated uncoupler. It has a latch which opens the knuckle when a magnet pulls the uncoupling pin downward. A coil is installed under the track to do this. This coupler has the advantage that false uncoupling doesn't occur if a train should slacken accidentally when passing over a ramp. The Marco knuckle stays open until recoupled. For that matter, cars cannot couple unless at least one of the pair of knuckles is open in advance. See Fig. 13-5.

Fig. 13-7. The Kadee coupler gauge in use. "Air hose" on coupler should just clear bottom extension on gauge.

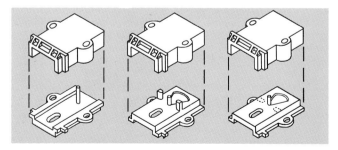

Fig. 13-8. Cover plate of PFM-Kemtron six-way coupler pocket (sometimes called draft gear) is turned to accept Mantua couplers at left, other types at center. In some cases the side pins must be lopped off as at right. Two size 0 screws ¼" long or cement can be used to mount the box. Cement may eventually loosen and allow box to drop.

Coupler maintenance

MDC and dummy couplers

A model of a real railroad coupler almost true in HO scale is the Roundhouse coupler made by Model Die Casting. The knuckle operates in the same manner as that on a real railroad coupler, after the locking pin is pulled manually. Automatic uncoupling is not practical.

Dummy-type couplers are similar and made by several makers. They do not have a moving knuckle so you couple cars by lifting one coupler over the other. You can file the contour of the dummy so it will fit with other makes and also with Kadee couplers.

The dummy and Roundhouse couplers' chief advantages are in looking more like real couplers than any others. They are often used on prize contest models and by model railroaders who are not interested in switching.

Coupler maintenance

I have already mentioned some of the causes of coupler trouble, but since they are somewhat the same for all couplers I shall repeat some advice here. Couplers on ready-to-run cars are not always in proper condition when you get them. As with kit couplers and couplers bought separately, every coupler on ready-to-run cars should be checked.

First remove any feathery "flash" on the working edges of the couplers and inside their knuckles. Be sure to preserve the hook within the hook on both the horn-hook and knuckle-type couplers if you have to do any cleaning here. A small pointed model file will reach the areas inside the knuckle.

The working faces of the knuckle, gathering horn, and uncoupling pins should be smooth or even polished. If you use a file to do this smoothing, file horizontally rather than vertically so minute scratches will aid rather than impair the coupling action.

Next, check the coupler mounting. The coupler should be free to move to either side and the springs should return it to position quickly. If operation is not snappy, look for rough edges around or on the coupler shank and also see that the coupler pocket cover isn't too tight. If it is, file the coupler shank a little thinner.

On the other hand, if the coupler pocket is too roomy — a common fault with horn-hook couplers — you will have to make the cover plate fit more closely or else add a shim of smooth metal or celluloid to take up the space. A loose coupler will sag and rise up

too far or twist on its axis. This can cause the uncoupling pin to lift out of a ramp and also snag or even uncouple by touching switch rails and highway crossings. A too-long coupler pin will also do this; but never shorten the pin if the coupler itself is too low. Once the pin is clipped too short, it can never be used successfully in an uncoupling ramp.

The center of most types of couplers should be $25/64''$ above rail level. Get this right first. Then check to see that the uncoupling pin is between $1/32''$ and $3/64''$ above rail level. You can do this by laying a piece of model stripwood $1/32''$ thick across the rails and seeing that the pin grazes it.

Model Die Casting and Kadee make bumperlike devices (Fig. 13-7) for checking horn-hook and MKD couplers respectively, and you should not be without one.

When a coupler is found to be too low, you can add "truck washers" from the hobby shop to raise the end of the car. Place these as needed between the truck and the car bolster.

If a coupler is too high without washers, a rare occurrence fortunately, the coupler pocket must be shimmed down, or material must be filed from the body bolster above the truck. Don't file the truck, as it may not always be used on the same car.

Coupler side swing

Most couplers are swiveled so they stay coupled on curves. This need is greatest when a long car or engine enters a curve. The end of the loco swings far to the side and the coupler pivot is usually way outside of the outer rail. The next car, still on straight track, has its coupler pivot at track center. The working ends of these couplers must be able to swing to the side far enough that the couplers still join. If anything prevents this side play, the loco or car or both will derail. This type of derailment is most common with combinations of Athearn GP-9 locomotives and any freight car with Talgo-type trucks.* This is because this combination has the greatest and the least side swing on adjacent equipment. The plastic step on the GP-9 interferes with the location of the coupling pin on horn-hook couplers (Fig. 13-10) and so the step should be cut away as required. Fig. 13-9 shows that the coupler has proper side play when the body of the loco has been removed.

When you paint a car or locomotive, don't let paint get into the working parts of any coupler. The only suitable lubricant is graphite, which is easily applied in an alcohol suspension such as Neolube.

*These are the trucks with couplers mounted on them instead of on the cars as explained near the end of chapter 12.

Fig. 13-9. Proper use of a gauge for checking couplers is a necessity for consistently good operation. This one is made by MDC (Roundhouse) for horn-hook types. Kadee and Mantua make equally good gauges for their lines of couplers. Hidden uncoupling pin of this Athearn Geep's coupler has cleared platform P without stubbing its toe. Tips of both knuckle and gathering horn also come to proper places on gauge, so this coupler is okay. Every coupler should be checked. Unsuspected cause of trouble is sometimes truck mounting screw which allows whole engine or car to move too far to side, taking coupler with it.

Fig. 13-10. Coupler in Fig. 13-9 was checked with loco body removed. When body was replaced, step would not allow coupler to swing as far as required. This caused derailments of cars coupled to this engine on sharp curves. Part of the loco step had to be removed along dashed line.

14: Kit construction

SINCE all American-made HO kits and ready-to-run equipment (and some imported HO equipment as well) are made to work together on the same railroad, you have literally hundreds of kits to choose from in building cars, locomotives, and structures. Some of the kits are very well made; most are good; a few are only fair. The fair kits can be made into good models if you put enough of your own time and skill into their assembly. Sometimes you can improve a fair kit by merely replacing one or two crudely fashioned parts with better parts bought separately.

It is wise to start with what might be called "easy" or "simple" kits, not so much because you couldn't assemble the "hard" kits but rather because you will learn some important things that are not explained in the instruction sheets of the more advanced kits; also because you will gradually build your collection of tools and develop patience.

In the spring of 1957 I started keeping notes on the assembly of more than 200 kits of almost every type and make. I wanted to learn which kits were easiest for beginners, which presented special problems, and which took a long time to complete.* In the following list I have arranged a number of kits in their approximate order of increasing difficulty. They take from 10 minutes to 2 hours to assemble, require only 2 to about 10 basic tools, and have (in general) instruction sheets that are easy to follow.

Mantua freight and oldtime cars.
Varney plastic cars.
Roundhouse cars with plastic body.
Athearn cars.
Tru-Scale plastic cars.
Revell, Tru-Scale, and other plastic buildings.
Rosebud-Kitmaster and other imported plastic models.
Herkimer metal cars.
Mantua streamlined cars.
Tenshodo die-cast locomotive.
Penn Line diesel locomotives.
Bowser locomotives.
Athearn band-drive locomotives.
Athearn geared locomotives.
Hobbytown locomotives.
Rivarossi locomotives.
Tenshodo locomotive kits, brass.

Nearly all of these come already painted. The others are plastic, which is easy to paint by hand if you use a "styrene" type of paint. The Rosebud-Kitmaster cars and locomotives are in OO scale, a little larger than HO. It takes quite a while to paint them. This line is more of a "replica" line than one of working models, but British mechanisms are made for them.

In general, flatcars, gondolas, and simple buildings are easy to build; tank cars, cabooses, and buildings with many gables and windows are more difficult, or at least take longer to assemble. Most of the locomotives listed are easy to put together, but they are not as simple as the cars. The Penn Line diesel is perhaps the easiest of all locomotives to build.

More difficult kits fall into different groups. Kits in which wood is largely used are really easy to assemble except that they may take a long time to complete — typically, 6 hours — so

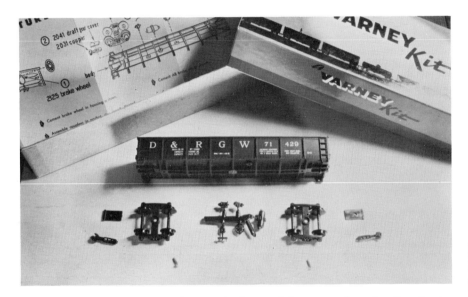

Figs. 14-1 and 14-2. This simple plastic gondola car took only 12 minutes to assemble; it required only two tools — knife and screwdriver — and cement.

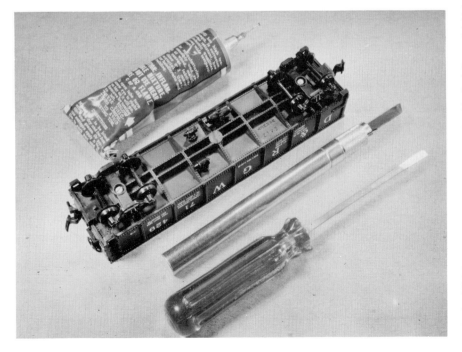

*The individual kits from this study were reviewed in the "Inspection Pit" department of MODEL TRAINS magazine. The emphasis of the reviews is on construction, performance, coupler installation, painting, and refinements you can add yourself. Back copies of many of the review issues are still available. There is a different type of review in MODEL RAILROADER magazine's "Trade Topics" department which deals with new kits, commenting frankly on their quality and value.

keep this in mind if you are the impatient type. Be sure to build a Campbell structure early in your program, for these kits have excellent instruction sheets and will help you figure out the other kits.

While I have tried to arrange this list in the order of increasing difficulty again, this is not so easy to do with wood kits, for the number of parts makes more difference than does the manufacturer.

Model Hobbies structures.
Dyna-Model structures.
Suydam structures, wood or card.
Campbell structures.
Main Line cars.
Suydam cars.
Ambroid cars.
La Belle cars.
Silver Streak cars.
Pacific HO cars.
Con-Cor cars.
LW Models cars.
Central Valley cars.
Cliff Line cars.
JC cars (metal sides).
Walthers cars.
Binkley cars.
Red Ball cars.

Metal kits are usually fairly simple except for requiring painting. Most of the realistic MDC (Model Die Casting) Roundhouse line of metal cars are in this class, as are the equally excellent kits by Ulrich, Model Engineering Works, etc. Typically, a metal car kit may require 3 hours or so for assembly and usually there's at least a half hour of flash-cleaning to do. More about this in a few moments.

I have not mentioned every make and by the time you read this the lists may have changed. This does not infer that unmentioned cars are any less suitable.

Traditionally the HO steam locomotive has had a die-cast boiler which has to be painted, and there has usually been a valve gear linkage which has to be riveted together. Recently there has been a trend to either prepainted boilers or plastic boilers (sometimes with a loss of pull because of reduced weight) and to assembling valve gear at the factory. These changes will put some steam-type locomotives near to, if not within, the "simple" class.

The traditional steam-type locomotive kit usually takes me from 3 to 6 hours to assemble. In some cases it is necessary to drill and tap holes or even cut away some metal. In my opinion the Mantua line is simplest for the first start on a steamer; then Varney; then Penn Line, Bowser, and Roundhouse as a group. I have found the Penn Line engines usually give the smoothest performance even though they may require a longer breaking-in period.

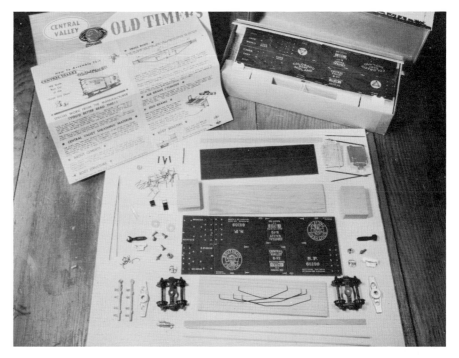

Fig. 14-3. Central Valley oldtime boxcar, a favorite of advanced modelers, has more parts than the simple gondola and takes at least 5 hours to build.

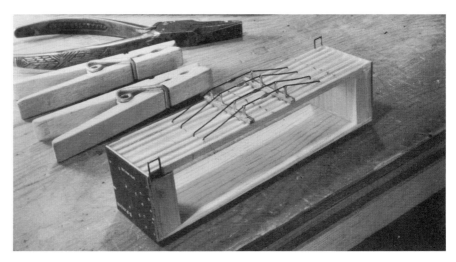

Figs. 14-4 and 14-5. One hour after beginning assembly of the boxcar, the roof, end blocks, floor, and outer end pieces have been cemented together and truss rods have been added. Two hours finds the couplers and bolsters, as well as the old-style brake cylinder fitting, in place. Now see Fig. 14-6.

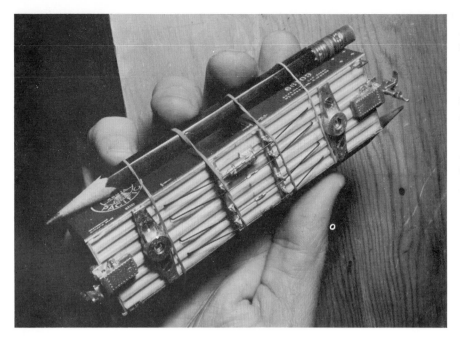

Fig. 14-6. Construction of the boxcar continues: A little later, pencils and rubber bands are used to hold the car sides in place while the cement sets.

Fig. 14-7. Three hours: Fascia boards have been attached; are now trimmed.

Fig. 14-8. Four hours: The ladders on this car were made by pushing grab-irons into holes drilled at the points printed on the car sides and ends.

Most (but not all) European-made copies of American steam-type locomotives are incorrectly proportioned, either having certain European characteristics such as slanted sides on the cab, or being to 4 mm. rather than 3.5 mm. scale (oversize by 14 per cent). Possibly such irregularities will be corrected by the time you read this. While it doesn't come in a kit, another size misfit is the Revell 0-6-0 tank switcher, which is much larger than HO scale even though it will run on HO track.

Some Japanese-made locomotives are also out of size; some have poor motors, some poor gears or universal linkages; but on the whole the Japanese imports have improved in quality year by year until the best are now superb.

I want to point out one or two more makes of HO kits. Suydam's metal industrial buildings require soldering, and this is a good place to learn the technique. Several firms make interesting cars and apparatus for modeling a lumbering branch line. Others offer equipment for interurban, streetcar, or heavy electric lines; and still others make kits for narrow-gauge lines. These are in HO scale but are called HOn3 because they run on scale 3-foot-gauge rather than standard-gauge track.

Most of the kit manufacturers also sell spare parts. It's good to have all the catalogs you can send for, just for these parts listings and the general information they give. I can't begin to list them all, but the following firms' catalogs of parts might be most useful to you: Northeastern (wood shapes), Kemtron, Cal-Scale, Selley, Model Die Casting, Model Engineering Works, Varney, Mantua, Red Ball, Walthers, Tru-Scale, Suydam, Craftsman Supply, etc. Some firms make a small charge for their catalogs. Such charges are usually listed in the advertisements in MODEL RAILROADER and other publications.

Routine for kit assembly

When you have the table cleared and have set out the kit and tools (see page 76), the next thing to do is look at the instruction sheet. You are supposed to read it through before starting construction. Often that will be the dullest 5 minutes of your day, for instruction sheets are rarely written in an entertaining manner. Since it will take extreme concentration to think about what you are reading, let me help you by telling what this reading is for: You want to be sure you don't do something you cannot easily undo. For instance, at the under edge of a Roundhouse metal boxcar roof there's a little ridge; you might think this is "flash" and file it off. But this ledge helps hold the ends on the car. And there you are, on a Sunday afternoon — you didn't read the instructions, you filed the ridge off, and now there's no hobby shop open for you to go to and get another roof.

Or you can be assembling a locomotive valve gear with tiny rivets, and you put one part on top of instead of below the other. Then you have to drill out the rivet to remove it and get the parts separated; if you do this more than once or twice you'll use up the spare rivets usually supplied in a kit.

So what you most want to see is that everything is in the right place before you *bend, rivet,* or *cement* anything together. Another thing to guard against is getting parts in place upside down, backwards, or out of correct order. Sometimes very small differences between two parts are not easily detected until after you have the model well along. You may put the wrong part in first and then have to take it out again.

Usually, the following order will be most convenient in kit assembly:

1. Clean flash from all plastic and metal die castings. (Flash is the feathery edge left at parting lines and inside openings where metal or plastic leaked into cracks in the mold. The older a mold gets, the more flash will be on the model castings it makes.)

2. Paint all small parts, stripwood, car ends, roof, underbody, etc., before assembly, if you can. This makes final painting only a matter of touch-up and also gives a cleaner paint job. (However, do not paint surfaces where cement or solder will be applied later.)

3. After this prepainting, assemble the main parts of the car. With metal cars this is usually done from the top down. With wood cars, the floor, end filler blocks, and roof are first cemented together and the remaining wood parts are then added.

4. Add grabirons, ladders, and the brake wheel.

5. Next add parts under the body, including couplers and trucks.

6. Check the coupler height (see page 42) and correct it now, if need be, before the car gets lost among others.

7. Touch up any parts that are still unpainted.

Painting with a brush can result in a sorry job, if you are not careful. Usually the paint should be about as thick as canned milk and you must apply it without dragging the brush through any half-dry places. If you do have to go back over some area, wait until the paint is entirely dry and then work quickly. It is a good idea to "weather" your cars if you hand-paint them, as the weathering hides brush marks. Get the effects of dust near the trucks and floor line; add spilled oil, cement, or streaks of rust near rivets and edges of metal. A little practice will make even ordinary cars look much more realistic. See page 50.

Of course, if you can afford an airbrush and some way of supplying the high-pressure air or gas to operate it, you can do an excellent paint job on your cars, engines, structures, and scenery. Excellent outfits sell for a little over $20 including airbrush, hose, valve, and canned gas. The Binks is one such gun.

Fig. 14-9. Completed car took almost 5 hours for assembly, another hour for paint touch-up. Few HO cars have lettering provided on end as this one does.

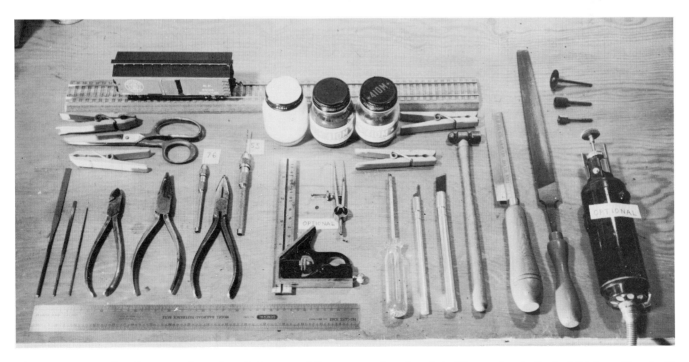

Fig. 14-10. I used quite a number of tools in assembling this car but you can get by with less. I also used cement and paint. The motor tool at right is optional. It speeds cutting wood and metal, and also drilling holes.

Painting and weathering

When you weather cars, look at real railroad cars frequently for ideas. Notice how few cars have weathered in the same way. Some cars have little grime; others are oily; still others are covered with powdery white dust or washes. Stock cars sometimes have a mixture of white lime together with spilled manure leaking out the sides along the floor line.

Here's a good pallet of colors for all kinds of weathering:

Effect	Colors to use
Rust	Burnt sienna, thick and thin.
Mud	Raw umber and white, or other earth colors and white.
Grease	Burnt umber, thick or thin. Also add black or blue to burnt umber.
Lime	White.
Manure	Raw sienna or light yellow ocher.

Floquil makes a weathering kit with essentially these same colors.

Any artist will notice that these are mostly "earth colors," which are merely ground clay with varying amounts of iron oxide in them for the color. These are by far the safest colors for weathering effects, and they really are dirt. You can use these colors in any type of paint, so select a kind you like to work with. Most liquid colors as used for models are fine for spraying and spattering effects. Spattering is when you flick a toothbrush of color at an engine or car to weather it. Spattering must be done with a lot of restraint.

I do the bulk of my weathering with an old artist's watercolor brush, say size 4, using artist's oil colors but thinning them with Floquil Diosol. This works better than to use turpentine because the work dries much faster. It does not seem to have any effect on undercoats of Roundhouse (MDC) or Floquil paints; thus your weathering can be wiped off if you want to try again.

First I wash on any colors that are supposed to look rain-washed or oil-streaked, using a rather dark but very wet mixture. This is also good for the powdery white effect seen on some boxcars. Flow the color on and let it drain down the sides of the model.

Next I smear drier weathering effects onto the car with a nearly dry mixture of paint and thinner. This is more like stenciling and can give various effects, including lime-and-manure near the floor line of a stock car.

Finally, if I use an airbrush at all, I spray on dusty effects, especially near the wheels, floor, and lower parts of the car end. Floquil's color "Earth" is very handy for this.

When weathering plastic cars, the thinner will craze their surfaces, and this is usually desirable; but be careful not to get the surfaces so wet they take more than a minute to dry or you get an uneven, icy-looking glaze.

If you don't want the thinner to affect the plastic surface at all, spray the car ahead of time with Floquil Glaze and let it dry for at least a day. Once dried, the Floquil Glaze will protect the plastic from other kinds of thinner long enough to get your weathering in place. This is because Floquil Glaze doesn't dissolve again, once it has really hardened — a handy property. Other model glazes will dissolve again.

Where there are rows of rivets or other metal edges, a touch of rust on each rivet gives a particularly fine effect. Also, you can paint slightly different hues of dirt on the panels of the roof. Try anything and also try to do each car a little differently than the others.

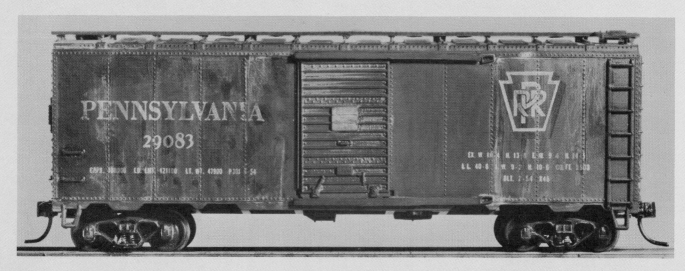

Any type of paint can be *sprayed* on plastic, metal, or wood models alike, as the coat is very thin. "Styrene" paints are the safest for *brushing* on most plastics, as ordinary paints may affect the surface, crazing it or producing an eggshell finish.

You might think the competitive makes of paint are all alike; actually, several have unique qualities. One of the oldest lines is Floquil; this has the fine quality of setting, not just drying. Once set (a matter of several days' standing after first drying), Floquil is very durable and can withstand additional coats of itself or other makes of paint without softening. Floquil can be baked for quicker setting. This make also has what I believe is the widest variety of colors.

Floquil's only fault is that it tends to coagulate in the bottle if not used up fairly soon after first opening the bottle. Floquil sells an excellent booklet, *Painting Miniatures*, that tells how to overcome this and gives other help on painting and weathering.

The paint called 410M comes in a regular type which I cannot recommend except for use on wood, as it doesn't adhere well to some metals. On the other hand, 410M Styrene paint is not only suitable for plastics, for which it is intended, but it seems to work well on metal and wood as well and is easy to handle.

For keeping quality and for easy mixing of special colors I like Roundhouse paints, made by Model Die Casting Co. You may have to order these by mail; I don't often see them in hobby shops. Quite a number of colors are made and they all handle well in an airbrush.

By now you probably realize that getting paint to stick to brass or other metals used in cars and locomotives isn't always easy. Some kinds of brass and zinc alloy seem to give more trouble than others, and I'm not sure anyone has found the universal answer.

At any rate, all grease should be rinsed off a model with any lacquer thinner, but preferably with the same kind of thinner that is going to be used later for the paint. After this, some zincs and brasses can be etched in oxalic acid or Metal-Prep, a material sold by automotive paint supply houses. As this etching step doesn't always help, I now skip it and instead coat the well-cleaned and dry model with watery-thin shellac. (Cut white shellac with equal parts of shellac thinner.) You can dip or spray the model to save time. Be sure you reach all the areas to be painted later.

It is too bad that the black-and-white photos on page 50 emphasize the artificial streaking of colors. In full color the effect is much more natural.

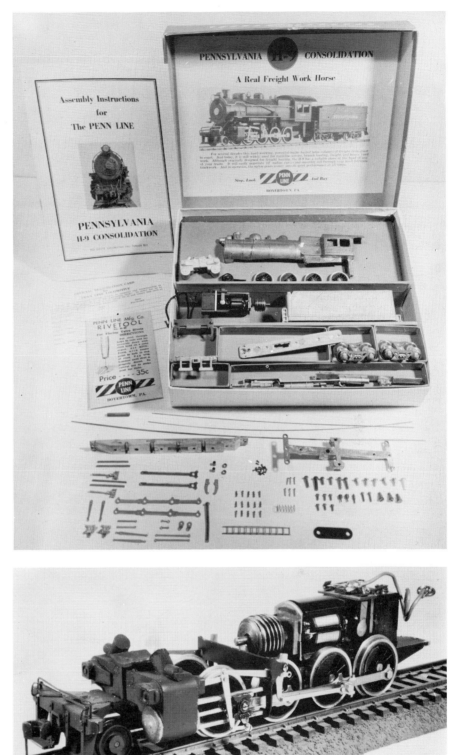

Fig. 14-11. It took me 6½ hours to assemble the Penn Line Consolidation locomotive kit, longer than average for a steam-type engine. In order that the model may negotiate sharp curves, the center drivers are flangeless.

Kit structures, a modified kit locomotive and scratch-built cars are combined in this scene on the Portage Hill & Communipaw Ry., a project of Kalmbach Publishing Co. The area shown is about 2 x 3 feet; it includes two legs of a wye track and a factory spur in the background. Scenery is made of plaster-soaked paper towels.

Clint Gran

This weathering job was done by Bill McClanahan, using oil colors thinned with turpentine. After the locomotive was painted, Bill streaked it with shades of gray, white, and rust-colored browns to make it look this way.

Ralph Baxa.

Something in this scene sets it apart from many others that show one track crossing over another: The lower track is not level with the surrounding terrain; it has been depressed to form what is actually a third level. This small detail is much more effective than just having the lower track level with the surrounding ground.

Most of the weathering and aging processes in this scene by John Novar are built right into the models. Note the nails, cracked and broken boards, irregular shingles. Models were built of stripwood which was then stained to simulate weathered wood rather than painted boards.

Along the right of way

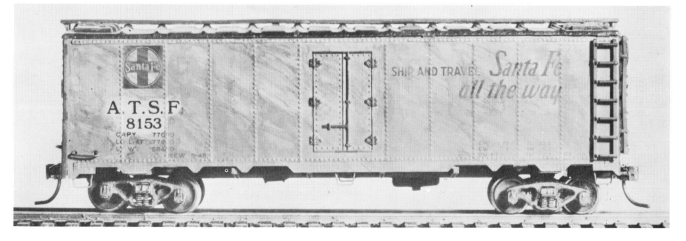

Linn Westcott used artist's oil colors to weather this Santa Fe refrigerator car model. An interesting feature is the manner in which the dirt has been wiped from the reporting marks as if it had been done by a yard clerk.

15: Wiring accessories

A MODEL railroad comes to life when you provide lights in the buildings, street lights along the roads and station platforms, smoke units in factory or other chimneys, and perhaps even add motor-operated accessories such as a loader, animated sign, old mill with waterwheel, merry-go-round in a small amusement park, working turntable, working highway flashing lights or operating crossing gates. Some of these things are made ready to install. For the others you can buy low-cost lamp bulbs, motors, and gears, and build your own.

How about the electric current to operate these things?

You must consider four things for each accessory you add:

1. What is its rated voltage?
2. Will it need a.c. or d.c.?
3. What will control it?
4. Will it overload my power supply?

Most of the ready-to-use accessories will operate on 12 v. d.c. or 16 v. a.c., as they are designed for the simplest possible connection to your power pack's accessory terminals. However, it is important to know the accessory voltage rating because if it is less than the pack supply voltage, you will burn out lamp bulbs quickly. Look on the package or ask your dealer.

Many of the larger and some smaller power packs have terminals marked "uncontrolled d.c." and "a.c." These usually provide around 12 v. to 16 v., which is usually just right for the ready-to-use accessories.

Accessories containing only lamp and smoke units can be operated on either a.c. or d.c., but it's a little easier on your power pack if you use the a.c. terminals for these devices. Fig. 15-1 shows the beginning of a string of lamps and a smoke unit and how they can be connected to the a.c. terminals. The on-off switch is really

optional and can be omitted if you don't mind having all of the accessories turned on all the time.

Occasionally an a.c. motor may be found in an accessory, but this is rare. In such a case, it should be added as shown in Fig. 15-2. This drawing also shows how groups of lamps and even an individual lamp can be turned on and off with separate electric switches.

Most motor-operated devices and some coil devices have to operate on d.c. In this case you use the same kind of a circuit but with the power coming from the uncontrolled d.c. terminals, as in Fig. 15-3. Notice here that I have added a switch for each motorized accessory, as you are quite likely to want to turn different devices on and off at different times.

In the same way, Fig. 15-4 shows exactly the same circuit, but instead of using individual toggles Atlas "Connector" devices are used. These are handy units that contain three on-

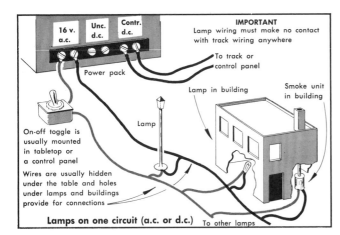

Fig. 15-1. Connect lamps and smoke units to a.c. power.

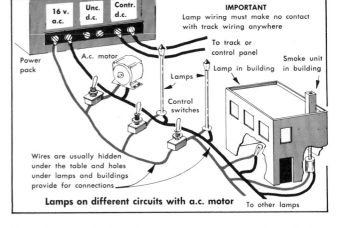

Fig. 15-2. Control motor, lamps, with separate switches.

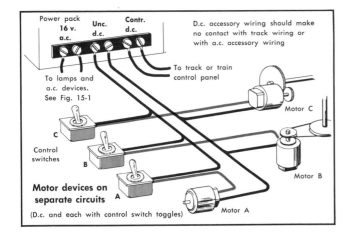

Fig. 15-3. Use uncontrolled d.c. for most model motors.

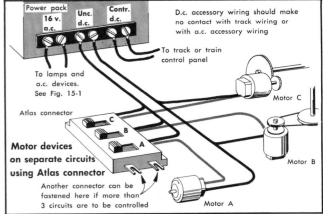

Fig. 15-4. Atlas connector used in a similar circuit.

Wire

Hobby shops carry several kinds of wire for making connections between power pack and track accessories. When several wires must go to the same place you can use ribbons of wire; these are handy, as they lie flat against the underside or even the top of your table. Each wire has its own color, a help in making sure of your connections. For instance, in Fig. 15-8 it is important that wire B goes all the way back to the power source.

Colored wire is also available singly in various sizes and in two general types. "Solid wire" has only one piece of metal in its center. This is the easiest to use in small sizes, but in big sizes (such as size 14, used in house wiring) it is not well suited to the wiring of small railroads. It has so much mechanical strength that it is likely to damage the things it is connected to.

Size 18 wire is better, but for most model railroad purposes smaller size 20, 22, or even 24 wire will handle all the current you will need and be much easier to use.

The other kind of wire is "stranded wire." It is made of a number of small wires bundled together inside a layer of insulation. Stranded wire is the only type to use in places where the wire must be flexible (inside locomotives, for instance; or where making connections to a movable control panel, or a lift-out track bridge). Once the connection is made, stranded wire will stand up better mechanically because of its flexibility.

I use a great deal of wire called "indoor antenna wire" which is available in radio stores and in some hobby shops. This is size 25 and is very flexible. Years ago we thought this size was too small, but in many places it is ideal for HO wiring — in locomotives, control panels, and even to track and accessories within 10 feet or so of the control panel.

Flexible stranded wire has one bad fault. When you fasten it under screw terminals it tends to spread away, and a single strand may touch the next terminal and cause a short circuit.

Be sure to read in chapter 18 about running wires from track and accessories to the control center.

you'd better consult the installation sheet for specific instructions.

For automatic signal operation plus automatic stopping of a train at a red signal, consider the Tru-Scale line of signaling devices. Fig. F on page 45 of the book *How to Wire Your Model Railroad* also shows this scheme.

While the diagrams show the control toggle switches in a group near the power pack, this is merely to get the wiring scheme idea over to you. The length of wire and locations of the toggles can be changed any way you want for your convenience.

If a d.c. permag type motor is used for some accessory, you may want to reverse the motor at times. This might be the case in a motor operating an elevator or mine skip, or a motor operating a loading crane. Reversal is then accomplished in the same manner as for an HO locomotive. Fig. 15-5 shows how to do this with a toggle switch of the special dp. dt. co. (double-pole, double-throw, center-off) type. Below this the same thing is accomplished with an Atlas Twin, but in this unit there are two more terminals and another switch so you could also reverse a second motor device. Mantua-Tyco makes a handy reverse switch that reverses a motor only as long as you press a button.

If you wish to control the speed of a d.c. accessory motor, take the power from the "controlled d.c." terminals of the power pack. These are the same terminals that go to your track or control panel. You can arrange a switch so the track can be momentarily disconnected and the accessory motor connected while you control it.

Another and better scheme is to buy a low-cost power pack with speed control just for the accessory. This will usually have a built-in reversing switch and will cost from $5 to $10.

Power packs contain rheostats that are designed to control the motors in trains. These motors draw from .25 a. (ampere) to 1 a. or more. Motors which have an easy load may not draw this much current, and then the rheostat in a power pack may not be

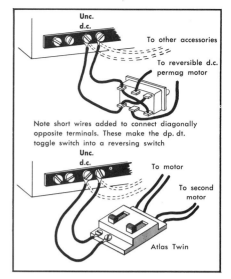

Fig. 15-5. Motor-reversing switches.

Note short wires added to connect diagonally opposite terminals. These make the dp. dt. toggle switch into a reversing switch

able to fully stop the accessory motor without a jerk. In this case buy a 10 ohm, 25 watt resistor from the hobby shop or a radio parts store and connect it across the wires to the easy-running motor, as in Fig. 15-6. This merely draws extra current so the power pack control behaves as though it were handling a bigger motor load.

How many accessories can one use? About 10 lamps take 1 a. of current, although the exact amount differs with different makes of lamps. Your power pack can usually handle 1 a. or so of accessories from the a.c. terminals in addition to the normal load of the train. Accessories requiring d.c. are just a little more of a load for your pack. In general you can count 1 a. for each train operated from a given pack, 1 a. for each 10 lamp bulbs, and perhaps ½ a. (a rough guess) for each motor-operated accessory. Add this up and be sure it does not exceed the ampere capacity of the power pack which the manufacturer claims for it.

The idea is not to overload the pack. Since the danger of overloading is overheating, one clue of an overloaded power pack is when it shows signs of getting more than slightly warm.

off switches each. They make it unnecessary to drill holes in a control panel for mounting the individual toggles. Your dealer may have still other kinds of on-off switches and devices; the shape may be different, but the electrical principle is usually the same.

The electric toggle switches just discussed are all worked by hand. There are also contact devices you can attach to the track so a lamp, signal, or motor device will operate when the train reaches a certain point. Again, the principle is the same but

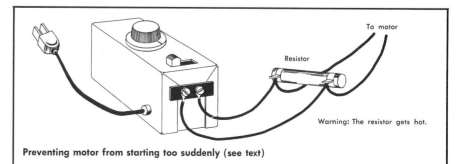

Preventing motor from starting too suddenly (see text)

Fig. 15-6. By dissipating some current as heat, the resistor controls motor.

Remote-control switches

Fig. 15-7. Tru-Switch with switch machine, its controller, and three-wire cable to connect the controller to the switch machine for remote control.

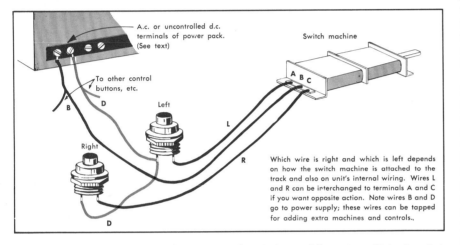

Fig. 15-8. Pushbutton circuit to control switch machine at a distant point.

I'm being a little unspecific here because there are so many sizes of power packs and so many kinds of accessories. However, I can assure you that burned-out power packs are not very common in our field, because of their protective circuit breakers, their rugged design (better makes at least) and because, if anything, the new model railroader is overcautious.

If you find that turning on accessories tends to slow your train or dim lights noticeably, get another power pack and divide the load.

You don't have to buy another power pack for lamps, just a transformer of the proper voltage. This is because the kinds of lamps we use most work just as well on a.c. as on d.c. Some hobby shops have or can order transformers for you. They cost less than power packs because they are not nearly so complicated inside.

You can save money on lamps by using those that operate on less than 12 v. Various voltages are made. These lamps cannot be powered directly from your power pack unless it has 6 v. or other special terminals.

The book *How to Wire Your Model Railroad* goes into this subject better than we have space to do here.

One of the most intriguing features of model railroading is the use of remote control to operate track switches. Certainly, you should consider adding remote control to any turnouts (track switches) which are not easy to reach while operating trains. Some model railroaders (in fact, I'd say a majority) also put remote control on turnouts that are close by, just because they like to. This is a matter of what you want to spend your money for. If you have many visitors there is also the advantage that with remote-control turnouts the visitors are less likely to get their hands in places where they can damage your scenery or derail trains.

The manufacturers of sectional track offer reasonably priced "switch machines" which attach to the turnouts or even come already built-in. In the beginning it is probably best to stick with these, but there are also special types of switch machines by other manufacturers that many ad-

vanced workers prefer to use. The advanced types are discussed in *How to Wire Your Model Railroad*.

The simpler switch machines are controlled and powered through three wires. You can buy special three-conductor flat cables or use three separate wires. Fig. 15-7 shows one type of switch machine and its controller.

Inside the switch machine are two coils of wire and an iron plunger that can slide inside from one coil into the other. If electric current is sent through one coil, it produces magnetism and the plunger is attracted. A lever or cam arrangement transmits the motion to the "points" of the track switch. By energizing one coil or the other the turnout is operated for either the straight or curved branch.

The coils are not able to withstand more than a few seconds of current without getting excessively hot. For this reason, only pushbuttons or other types of control devices that send current only briefly are used to control switch machines.

Fig. 15-8 shows how two pushbuttons (doorbell or similar) would be connected to control a switch machine. Many kinds of switch machine control devices are made and the hobby shop will probably have one or two types the owner considers good. Regardless of the shape, the principle of sending momentary current is the same, and each make of switch machine control comes with a wiring diagram which you will recognize as essentially the same as the one we've drawn here.

Since switch machines use current only momentarily, you do not have to allow for them when considering a power pack or transformer.

Most machines will work on either a.c. or d.c. in spite of the fact that the instruction sheet may indicate one or the other. A.c. is preferable if operation is satisfactory. A.c. also tends to make the machine vibrate, and this vibration can loosen a machine that has a stiff action. On the other hand, you may find operation a little more powerful and quieter with d.c.

If the plastic cover of a switch machine gets too hot, it will melt out of shape. Also, if a coil is energized for too long a time, it will burn out. Neither of these things can happen if your wiring is properly done and if the controller is in good condition. Sometimes a contact on a cheaply made switch machine control box will weld itself in the "on" position; this can burn out the coil. Outside of the cost of replacement, you will probably have little damage. But just to be on the safe side, be on guard for malfunctioning switch machines and control buttons. In a rare instance, a hot machine might start a fire.

Along the right of way

Larry Schreiber, like some other model railroaders, operates his pike from a control panel in the center. The idea is especially helpful on railroads that are too wide to permit reaching all parts of it comfortably.

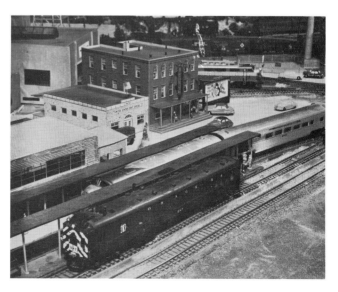

Good control systems are important when yards get as cluttered as this, with a switcher breaking up one train and another coming in. The F-3 diesel on Boyce Martin's Osage RR. is on its way to Lenbrook, where some of its cars will be transferred to the Nawsuh, Yewall & Shonuff, a short branch line. In the other scene on the Osage, a gas-electric waits in Helena for passengers from the streamliner just now coming into the station.

16: Simple control for two trains

HARDLY anyone who learns about HO railroading will be able to resist getting more than one locomotive and adding some turnouts (track switches) into the track pattern. But just as soon as you have two locomotives you have an electrical control problem. You can put both locos on the same train to haul more cars (providing each loco has about the same speed under load), but what do you do when you want to run two trains?

One thing you can do is to run the trains one behind the other on the same track. This works until one train catches up to the other.

You can isolate a part of the track into a "block." See Fig. 16-1. This block has a toggle or other type of on-off switch connected to one rail, and insulated plastic rail joiners in that same rail at the block boundaries.

What good is this?

Well, if one train begins to overtake the other, wait until it gets into this block and then flip the toggle off. This stops the racing train and gives the slower train a chance to make up some headway. After the trains are again well spaced, you can let the fast train run again by reflipping the toggle. I located this stopping block at the near side of the oval. Actually, you can do this in any part of any track plan. Only one rail has to have the insulated rail joiners. There are some other ways to do it in which both rails get insulated joiners.

I've labeled the rails S and N for South and North. This is a common practice in HO. However, the North rail has nothing to do with the world's North Pole. The N rail is usually the inner rail of the oval.

Notice the jumper wire from the S rail connection at the power pack to the toggle that controls the block. We connected to the S side only because we put the insulated joiners in the S rail. In this way, when the toggle switch is turned on the train never knows there's a block. But turn the switch off and the train stops right away, or as soon as it gets into the block.

May I make a suggestion?

Do exactly what we've done here before you read any further about two-train control. If electricity is new to you, this simple experiment may save you hours or days of frustration because the things you will read further on will be so much easier to understand after you have installed one stopping block just like this one.

The on-off switch can be a toggle

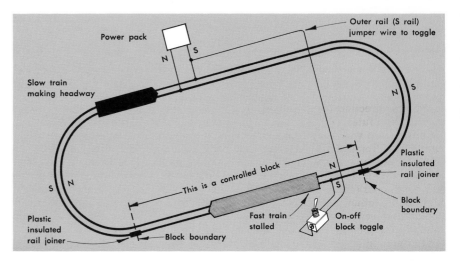

Fig. 16-1. Controlled block permits one train to stop while other continues.

as shown or you can substitute any kind of electrical on-off switch that is rated to handle 1 ampere or so of current. The voltage rating of a switch used in model railroading is not important.

A block like this one can be used to preset conditions so a train will stop when it gets to a station, to prevent a train from entering a yard or other busy area until it is wanted, or for many other useful reasons.

Selective-control turnouts

The turnouts called Tru-Switch (made by Tru-Scale) and some of the imported track switches have built-in contacts that accomplish the same result but in another way. In Fig. 16-2 a passing siding is shown. If you add this to your railroad and make it long enough to hold a train, you can stop a train on the passing track while another train goes by on the adjacent track. If you use Tru-Switches, one at each end of the siding, you need no special wiring at all. These turnouts have built-in contacts so that you can throw the turnouts for the main line just as soon as a slow train gets into the siding. This will automatically cut off the power and stop the train there until the faster train has passed on the main track.

Of course, you can do this with

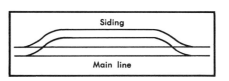

Fig. 16-2. Siding, or passing track.

other makes of turnouts too if you put two insulated rail joiners in one of the siding rails and add a toggle, as we did in Fig. 16-1. This makes a block out of the siding where you can hold a train regardless of the type of turnouts used.

This selective-control turnout is also handy in a yard arrangement, as in Fig. 16-3. In this scheme the hidden wiring in the Tru-Switch automatically cuts power from all the yard tracks unless a particular track is lined up to go out to the main. You can have a locomotive standing on each yard track, yet only one of them will start when you apply power.

Atlas and others provide other ways to accomplish these same feats, and it is a good idea to try each of several such schemes on your railroad. Each scheme has its own advantages and there's no reason to stick to only one manufacturer's products.

Two trains on separate routes

Most of what we've just talked about involves only one train running some of the time. One way to run two trains at the same time is to provide two separate routes. There are many track patterns of this type. Sometimes the routes are laid out like double track, Fig. 16-4, sometimes like entirely separate track, or sometimes a combination of each, Fig. 16-5.

A good way to wire these plans and any others with two separate routes is to use a separate power pack for each route. Another way is to use a two-throttle pack, but before you do this read about them in the first sections of this book. At any rate, we now have the ability to control both

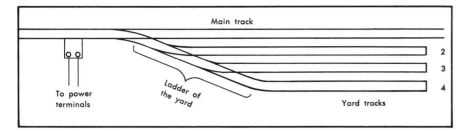

Fig. 16-3. Yard arrangements like this are easy with selective control.

speed and direction independently on each of the routes.

Usually you will want two pairs of connecting crossovers so a train can change from one route to the other or back again. In order to keep the rails from connecting from one route over to the other and causing electrical interference, you *must* put insulated rail joiners in *both* rails at each crossover.

One fault of this system is that a train may stall when going through either crossover because it straddles the separate territories of the two power packs. This is easily corrected. Notice the jumper wire J from the feeder wire going to the N rail of each power pack. Adding this interconnection will usually prevent such stalling.

Another cause of stalling when

crossing over is even simpler — perhaps you didn't line up the reversing switch properly so both sections of track will operate in the same direction!

That jumper wire J must not be used with the lower-cost two-throttle power packs because these packs, warned about in early chapters of this book, have internal connections that make external connections, like jumper J, prohibited. Jumper J actually produces what the experts call a "common-rail power return" system of wiring, usually called "common rail." That's nothing to worry about, however, and a lot of unnecessary copy has been written about "common rail" that only tends to confuse. Common rail is a wonderful scheme of wiring but requires no special considerations. You will get it automatically if you follow some of the better ways to power and control two trains.

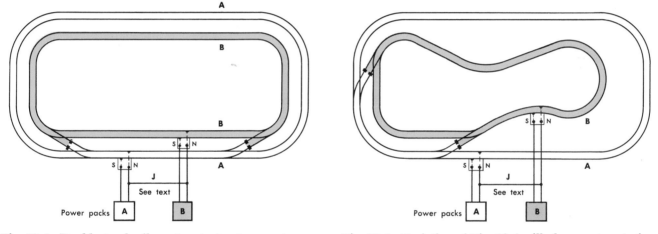

Fig. 16-4. Double track allows two trains to run at once. Fig. 16-5. Variation of Fig. 16-4 will also run two trains.

17: Better control for two trains

YOU'VE seen that built-in or attached controls on the turnouts can make one branch track active while a train stands on the other branch track. We didn't go into many examples of this but you can work these out very easily just by buying the track switches and/or attachments and experimenting with them. If you want more specific examples, there are several pages of them in the book *How to Wire Your Model Railroad.*

At first you will be happy with the simple control schemes you can develop from the information in the preceding chapter. You know how to

create a stopping block and you know that you can use more than one such stopping block, locating each wherever you wish. After you have experimented a little, you will find there are certain shortcomings in these simple control systems. However, through experiment you will learn, and a little more reading or careful rereading will clear up the puzzles.

For instance, when a train goes over the crossovers from one route to the other, Figs. 16-4 and 16-5, there will be a sudden change in speed. Often it will be a forward lurch and then speed will slacken. This is not only unreal-

istic and annoying, but if any of the cars happen to be passing over uncoupling ramps at the moment, they may part. Every time you back up, retrieve the train, and try again, the train still comes apart because of the jerky motion.

Isn't there some way to prevent this sudden changing of speed?

There surely is. Your trouble is that the train is responding first to the control setting of one power pack, then suddenly to the other. For a moment it gets power from both packs at once, usually producing a forward lurch. After this, it resumes more normal operation but at a new speed, unless you have taken care to set both packs for exactly corresponding speeds.

The trick is to do what the experts do. Always control a particular train from the *same* power pack. Even though the train is going into new territory you can still control it from the old-territory pack. Take a look at Fig. 17-1. This is the same as the previous drawings except for one feature. We've added an sp. dt. toggle (or other kind of switch with at least equivalent connections). With the switch thrown to the right we have the same connections as before. But we've shown the switch thrown to the left, and if you carefully trace the route of the connections you will see that this connects the inner oval as well as the outer to pack A. For the moment pack B is out of use. The new switch allows us to select either pack A or pack B for powering that inner oval. Now when we run a train from the outer track to the inner there will be no jerking, no change in speed, because the train is getting power from the same power pack all the time. We didn't have to put any switch in the feeder wires to the N rail of the inner oval because this rail already had a direct connection via jumper J which we installed in the last chapter.

As we noted, pack B is idle for the moment but it could be connected through additional toggle or other kinds of switches to separated parts of the track for running another train somewhere else. This is exactly what we're going to do next.

For a moment, however, let's diverge to another problem, one created by what we have done to this point.

Suppose you are running one train on the outer oval and another on the inside. You want the outer train to cross over to the inside, so you throw the toggle, Fig. 17-1. This is fine for the train that's going to cross to the inner track, but you've suddenly shifted all the inner track to the same power pack and now you have both trains running from pack A. That's not good because our whole object is to keep the control of trains separated. Obviously, we need something more.

Control blocks for all trackage is better

What we need are a lot of "control blocks." A block is an electrical island in the track wiring — a place where you can do something to the running power that won't affect the rest of the railroad. We created a single "stopping block," Fig. 16-1, with no power and it stopped a train without affecting the rest of the railroad. If we could now connect this same block to a second power pack, we could run a train at one speed in this block while the rest of the railroad was set for other speeds or even the opposite direction. Our "stopping block" can now have independent control; it becomes a "control block."

From now on, most of the track wiring you do will involve these very basic and simple principles:

1. Divide *all* of your railroad into separated blocks so that no matter where one train goes it can have separate control from any other trains.

2. Be able to shift the connections of any power pack to any part of the railroad at your convenience. (No permanent connection to any particular part of the track.)

3. Provide as many sets of speed and reversing control devices (cabs) as there are trains in simultaneous operation. That is, if you plan to run three trains at the same time, you will have at least three speed controller levers or knobs — in effect, a "throttle" for each train. Each of these will have its own associated reversing lever. You don't need four sets of speed control and reversing devices unless you are actually going to run four trains at the same time, etc. This is where you'll begin to save money and have better control at the same time.

Now look at Fig. 17-2. Here's another double-track railroad, but the track plan could be *any* track plan. We've shown the plan divided into eight separate blocks by putting insulated rail joiners in both rails at each place where one block ends and the next begins. The number of blocks is unimportant other than having enough so two trains never need to share the same block at the same time. Notice that each block has a terminal section (homemade connections or clip-on terminal connectors can also be used), and that we've assigned a number to each block. There are no hard rules for numbering, but I have numbered the inner blocks 1, 2, 3 and 4, and the outer blocks 11, 12, 13 and 14. It isn't necessary to have the blocks divided the same way on the inner and outer ovals, but doing so avoids confusion for visitors.

I have purposely omitted most of the track-to-control-panel wiring in Fig. 17-2 to show you the idea without confusion. Two wires are run from block 1 terminal track section to the control panel. Same again for block 11. No matter how many blocks you have, you keep on doing this until each block has its own pair of wires.

The control panel can be of any of many kinds of design. I've shown the map type with toggle switches, as it is one of the best types if you have the space for it. The diagram is made by using narrow colored adhesive cloth tape or paper masking tape to repre-

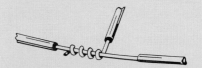
sent the track and cutting through the tape at each place where blocks end. You then bore holes in the panel front and insert a toggle or other type of switch for each block. Half-hard or tempered hardboard, such as Masonite, makes a good panel material.

In a smaller space, toggles could be mounted in a row. If you want to make the panel quickly, you can save time by using Atlas control devices or their equivalent. We'll discuss these in a moment.

Notice on this panel that the toggle handles point to left, right, or center. As we've drawn them, toggles for the inner oval are all flipped to the left. Thus all blocks on this oval are at the moment connected to the left-hand "cab" or power pack controls, cab A. In the outer oval, toggles for blocks 11 and 12 are shown in their middle or off positions while the remaining blocks happen to be connected to pack B at the moment.

From this you can see that you can instantly assign any block to either power pack or you can turn the power off in the block. This allows you to op-

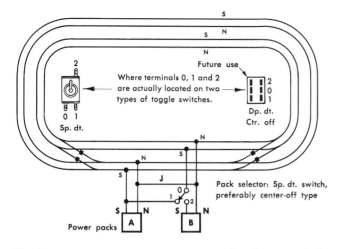

Fig. 17-1. How to connect a power pack selector switch.

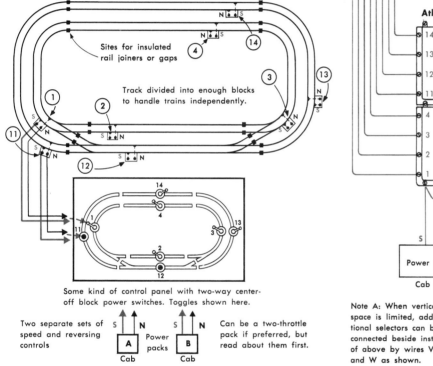

Fig. 17-2. How to wire a railroad for control of blocks.

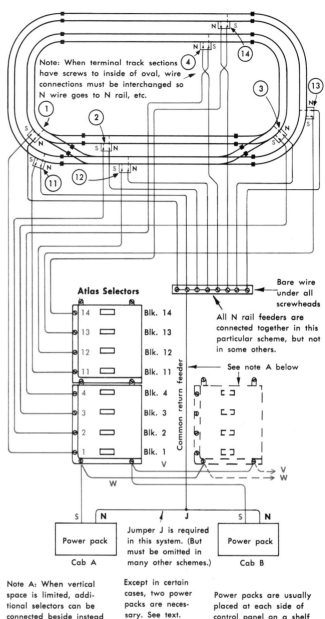

Fig. 17-3. Atlas Selectors for an eight-block railroad.

erate in many ways, two of which are explained here.

One way is to divide the railroad into divisions with high-speed blocks and low-speed blocks, using one power pack setting for one speed and the other pack for another speed. As trains are to be speeded up or slowed, you merely flip toggles so the blocks involved are shifted to the faster or slower power pack setting. This makes it particularly easy for one man to handle two and even more trains.

The other method is what this scheme was actually devised for, "cab control." This control can be used when you have more than one person operating a model railroad. With cab control you assign to each man one train, one throttle and reverser. His controls are his "cab." Now, no matter

where he runs his train, the man at cab A flips the control panel toggles so the blocks the train runs through are always connected to his own cab. He flips the toggles before his train enters any new block so there's no jerking of the engine.

The man at cab B does the same thing with his train, flipping the toggles as needed to the opposite side so his train is always powered from his power pack.

When operating in this way, it is a courtesy to flip toggles you no longer need back to center so the other fellow can see you are through using the particular block.

When you have a visitor you can do all the toggle flipping until the visitor gets the idea of it. The biggest problem for a visitor is learning where the

beginnings and ends of your various blocks are located. To help him, install signals or hang an imitation transformer on the nearest telephone pole, or use some other kind of an indicator that tells him where one block ends and the next block begins.

Atlas control devices

In the chapter on switch machine and lamp controls we discussed the use of the Atlas Control Box and Atlas Connector devices for operating turnouts by remote control and for switching on lamps and other accessories. The Atlas line contains other devices, and all are designed so one item slips into the next, reducing the amount of wiring and eliminating soldering. Other advantages are quick application, reasonable cost, no holes to drill except to guide mounting screws, and compactness.

For block control, Atlas makes devices called the "Twin," the "Controller," and the "Selector." Atlas also sells a book, *Wiring Your HO Layout*, to promote the use of these devices. The circuits in the Atlas book work, but I would like to suggest a different plan when it comes to block control, mainly because the device called the "Controller" is very confusing to use. You can do better by confining your track control wiring to the use of the "Selector" as shown in this chapter and adding the "Twin" as shown in a following chapter.

The complete hookup for an eight-block railroad is shown in Fig. 17-3. Each four blocks of the railroad are switched by an Atlas Selector unit. You can add any number of these four-block units. Unnecessary blocks may be left unused.

The Atlas literature shows these selectors mounted in a horizontal row; this has an advantage and a disadvantage. The advantage is that a wide control panel is usually easier to provide space for than a deep one. On the other hand, it is not easy to remember to slide the selector knob up for the power pack on the left and down for the one on the right. For that matter, the Atlas instructions show both power packs at the left, a very inconvenient arrangement when you are railroading with a friend.

My suggestion is to mount the selectors in a vertical row as shown. In this way the selector knob moves to left or right to select the power pack at left or right. If there is enough depth, you can mount more than one selector in the vertical row. If the vertical space is limited, merely add wires V and W and start one or more rows to either side of the first.

As mentioned earlier, the Atlas wiring system cannot be used with two- or three-throttle power packs unless there are no internal connections between the two or three power outputs. The MRC line includes two two-throttle power packs, and the higher-quality one, the "Dual Loco Pack," is safe to use. At this writing I know of no other suitable two-throttle pack.

When you use two separate packs, they will be more convenient if you mount one at each side of the control panel area. I have shown them below in these diagrams only to help in making the drawing fit the page space and to make the wiring more understandable.

How to handle a return loop, etc., will be handled in chapter 19.

Toggle-type control panels

While the internal wiring of a control panel is actually the same when

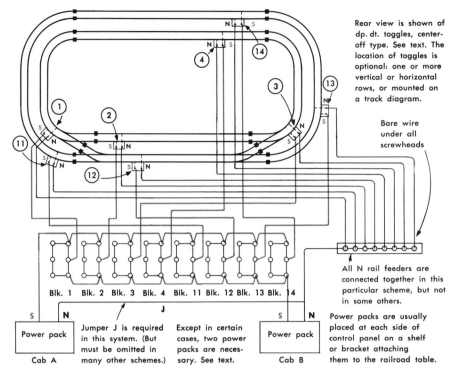

Fig. 17-4. **Complete hookup for an eight-block railroad using toggle switches.**

you use toggle switches, it looks more complicated because toggles are not made to slip one into the next as are the Atlas components.

The wiring using dp. dt. co. type toggle switches (sold in almost every hobby shop) is shown in Fig. 17-4. This scheme shows the toggles in a straight row, but you can mount them any way you like. If you have enough space, the map-type panel mentioned earlier is usually preferred.

Note that one wire from each power pack makes exactly the same connection to every toggle. The middle wire from each toggle is the one that goes to the track.

The common power-return wire

In both Figs. 17-3 and 17-4 the wires from the power packs to the N rail side of the track did not enter the control panel at all. Instead, the N rail wiring was all tied together via

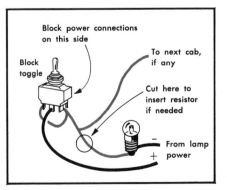

Fig. 17-5. **Wiring for a panel lamp.**

jumper J, below, and the terminal strip at the right. This terminal strip can be bought in either screw or solder terminal style. In either case, you should run a bare wire from one end to the other, making a good contact to each terminal connecting point. This provides a better way of joining eight or more wires into one than you could do without the terminal strip. Since all N wires are joined, it is not necessary for any particular wire to go to any particular terminal.

The idle contacts

At the left side of each toggle in Fig. 17-4, you'll note that three of the toggle terminals are not in use. They are not needed in this particular wiring scheme. However, if you like, you can put them to use to control panel lamps mounted to show which blocks are in use. The wiring for just one such block lamp is shown in Fig. 17-5. When the toggle is thrown to either right or left, the lamp goes on, showing the block is in use. Additional lamps can be added at some distance from the panel if you want to show that a block is in use in any part of the room.

It might occur to you that you could use this for signal control, and you could. It would not be exactly correct, however, because you would be turning the power on before the train reached a signal rather than as it passed one.

The power for panel indicator lamps should be of the proper voltage for the lamps, as discussed in chapter 15.

18: Block wiring for simple plans

THERE is a lot of help available for planning the blocks you will need on any large model railroad. The book *How to Wire Your Model Railroad* goes into every detail, and most of the plans in track plan books have been divided into blocks for you. But chances are that your first track plan will be fairly simple and maybe all the information you will need will be in this short chapter. Some of it is a review of things already mentioned.

First let me point out what you may already know about the block idea. You could compare a track plan in a crude way to a patio pavement. You can build a patio on a single slab of cement, or you can build it with many smaller tile blocks. Each block is independent to itself and normally doesn't touch any other tile, yet you can walk easily all over the patio.

In a way, a railroad divided into blocks is like the tile patio. A train can run all over the railroad, yet at any given time it is supported by only one block, or perhaps passing from one block to the next.

Each of our blocks will be a portion of track completely isolated electrically from the next block up and down the main line and isolated from important branch tracks as well.

The block is electrically isolated so you can run a train at one speed in one block regardless of what's happening in any other block.

Each block is therefore divided by boundaries from *all* adjoining blocks and at each place where we've chosen to put a boundary we will put insulated rail joiners or cut gaps in *both* rails. The experts can point out that in some places you may need insulation in only one of the rails, but putting insulation in both rails at every block boundary does absolutely no harm and eliminates the chance of making a mistake.

If the block is isolated from all others, it has to get power somehow. Thus, somewhere in the block there will have to be a terminal section or some other kind of electrical connection to the rails. The two wires, one for each rail, will have to go to the power pack. Just before these wires get to the power pack one or both of them will pass through an electric switch so this particular block can be switched on or off. In better control panels the block can also be switched to different power packs. That's what we did in the previous chapter and will do again in the next chapter.

Well, those are the essentials and now we have two problems: What are the practical ways to create these blocks, and just where and how many blocks shall we create? Let's start with the mechanical problems first.

After you have decided where a block boundary should go (instructions coming up soon), you can install plastic insulated rail joiners in place of the original metal joiners in both rails as the track is being laid down. However, if the track is already fastened down it is usually more convenient to saw through both rails. This is easy to do with a razor saw much as we trimmed track to length in chapter 7. The difference is that here we're merely slicing into rails that are going to remain in place.

A small block of wood can be held so it not only prevents the saw from wandering sideways as you start the cut, but also braces the rail from the pressure of the teeth.

After cutting through both rails, remove any loose particles of metal and dress any rough edges with a file. Check to see that the rail ends don't touch, and then squirt a little Ambroid or other quick-drying cement into the gap so that on some hot day rails won't expand and touch.

Use rail joiners or cut gaps at all block boundaries. Many blocks will have more than two boundaries.

Now for the feeder wires. If you are laying new track, you can usually use a terminal section. These come

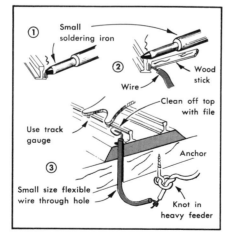

Fig. 18-1. Soldering wire to rail: Tin rail side, then wipe iron and put it on top of rail. Hold tinned wire in place with wood stick; remove iron and let solder solidify. Track gauge prevents rail from shifting if plastic ties soften from heat. The hotter the iron, the less the ties will soften, because the job will go faster.

in both straight and curved forms. Tru-Scale makes a straight terminal section that is also a rerailer and looks like a highway crossing.

If the track is already down or there is no room for a terminal section, your dealer may have some clip devices which you can attach to the rails. If not, you'll have to solder the wire connections as in Fig. 18-1. In some ways this is best. Use one or two rail gauges from the hobby shop so rails don't shift out of place should plastic ties soften during the operation. First put a little rosin-core solder on the side of the rail as at 1. Then heat the rail above this point and push the end of the small connecting wire into the still melted solder. If the solder doesn't wet the wire, apply a little more rosin-core solder directly to the wire or get cleaner wire.

Large wire should not be soldered directly to rail. It is likely to cause damage by bending the rail if someone accidentally tugs at the wire or if the rail expands due to heat.

Run the two wires from each block to a central location where you plan to put the control panel. Number the blocks and label the pairs of wires somehow so you don't have to duck under the table to see which wires go to which places.

When you route the wires from track connections to the control panel location, follow this procedure: From the hole where the connections come down through the tabletop, run the wires directly to the nearest frame member under the table at a right angle to that member. At this point fasten the wire to the member, or the underside of the table, with a sling of tape, or use a wire loop or hook.

Do not run wires in diagonal beelines from terminal track hole to control panel. This saves little time in the long run and is very likely to result in frequent wire damage.

From the track connection point or accessory location the wires should parallel framework members this way and that until you reach the control panel site. Use hooks or loops every 2 feet or less to hold the wire within 2″ or 3″ of the underside of the tabletop. Leave 12″ to 18″ of extra length at the control panel end for future connecting convenience.

When several wires go to the same general area, they can share the same hangers much of the way.

It is a good idea to use one color for all wires that go to one side of the track and another color for the op-

Feeders usually located at end of block nearest control panels.

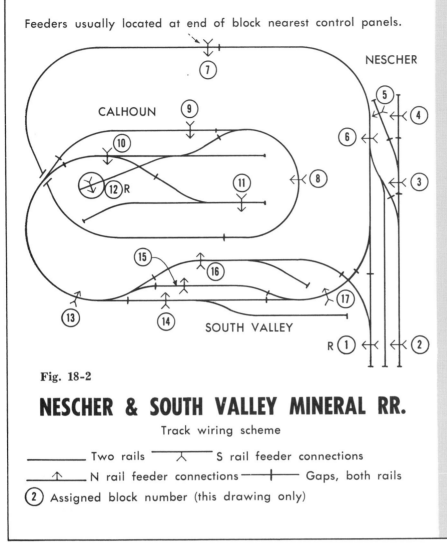

Fig. 18-2

NESCHER & SOUTH VALLEY MINERAL RR.

Track wiring scheme

———— Two rails ——⅄—— S rail feeder connections

——↑—— N rail feeder connections ——┼—— Gaps, both rails

② Assigned block number (this drawing only)

EXPLANATION OF BLOCK BOUNDARIES

① ⑫
These are blocks related to turntable and wye. Letter R indicates they should be powered via TURN controllers.
(Chapter 19)

② ⑪
Switchback spurs should usually be separated into their own blocks.

③ ④ ⑤
Short blocks are provided here so several engines can be stored and only one at a time moved out.

⑥
One yard lead forms block and also extends into any yard tracks where locos will not be stored — in this case, the middle track.

⑦ ⑰
Mainline block does not run into yard. This allows train to approach closer to NESCHER even though block 6 is in use for switching.

⑧
Short mainline block here allows switching at CALHOUN in same manner without interfering with block 7.

⑨ ⑩ ⑭ ⑮
Each passing track should be a block.

⑬
This mainline block was considered too short to break into shorter pieces, as were the blocks at each end of 7.

⑯
This track separated from 13 so train or engine can stand here.

posite rail. Perhaps you can use red for the S rail (outer) and white or black for the N rail (inner). Don't forget that on the far side of the oval the N rail is the one nearer you.

Where to make block boundaries

Well, now that we know what we're going to do, where do we do it?

You can lie awake nights worrying about this, but don't. No harm is done if you don't get the block boundaries in all the best locations, because changing boundaries is easy. New gaps can be cut and old unwanted gaps can be closed with metal rail joiners, plugs of solder, or (best) short jumper wires bridging across the gaps and soldered at each end.

The basic rule for locating blocks and their boundaries is this: *Have enough block boundaries so there is at least one boundary separating any two trains at all times.*

This sounds easy but it won't have much meaning for you until you see it in action.

Take an oval of track, for example. Suppose you want to run two trains

around it, one following the other. Will one block do? No, because both trains would be in the same block at the same time. Will two blocks do? Well, one train could be in one block and the other train in the other block, but they still couldn't go far because as soon as one train reached the beginning of the next block, it would be getting into a block with another train. You can get by with three blocks on any oval or circuit-type route, but four blocks are handier. In general, any route two or more trains are going to share should have at least twice as many blocks as there will be trains. Chalk up four blocks as minimum for any oval, and more if you're going to run more than two trains at once. If you have two ovals, each will need four or more blocks — a minimum of eight.

The next rule will cover many of your block situations automatically: *If you have any places where two turnouts point away from each other, close or far apart, you should put at least one block boundary somewhere between those turnouts.* Look carefully, for you may have more places like these than you think:

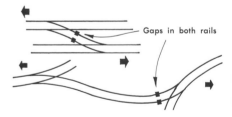

Now suppose you have one of the preceding situations where the turnouts are so far apart that you can get a train between them. In this situation you should put a block boundary close behind each turnout, creating a block between them:

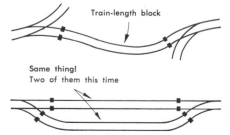

Notice how a passing track or double-ended yard track is the same thing, but doubled — each track needs two boundaries, four gaps per track. Be sure to also include gaps as needed for turning loops or wyes as described in chapter 9. These are most important.

Don't let this planning worry you — play it by ear but be willing to change the scheme when you find it will make it easier to run trains independently. Many published track plans, such as those in the book *101 Track Plans*, have the gaps and locations for terminal connections shown, and you can study these to see how many track patterns can be handled. The exceptions to the rules I've just given you are very few and mostly of a type where you'll hardly know the difference.

In general, however, be a little suspicious if you find gaps near the point end of a turnout like this:

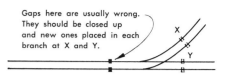

A convenient way to plan blocks is to put colored crosstie marks across a pencil sketch of your plan. Then check your work before actually cutting the rails.

Notice that we haven't worried about how many blocks we've created; we've been concerned only about block boundaries. This is quite proper and the blocks just happen.

Now if you count the isolated territories between the various block boundaries, you will know how many blocks you need to provide for on your control panel. A dozen or so is not uncommon on a small railroad. Assign each block a number.

Where do you put the track feeders? Each block will need a pair.

If you have done the preceding work properly, each block will have at least a part of its pattern as a single track. It may funnel out into several branches at one or both ends, but the trunk in the middle of this double-ended tree, or at the end of a single-ended tree, is a single track.

Put your feeder wire connections or terminal track wherever is most convenient on the rails that extend from this single-track part of the block:

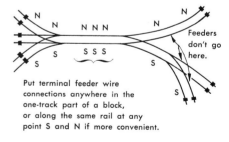

To see how one track plan worked out when following these rules, study Figs. 18-2 and 18-3.

If you have a return track such as a loop, wye, etc., as discussed in chapter 9, this must be a separate block for the very important reasons explained in that chapter. If the return section is big enough to hold two trains at the same time, then divide it into two blocks, etc.

Whether one block or more, add the letter R to the block number of all blocks in the return section, as we'll want to make special note of these later when building the control panel. You'll find published track plans usually show this R for your convenience.

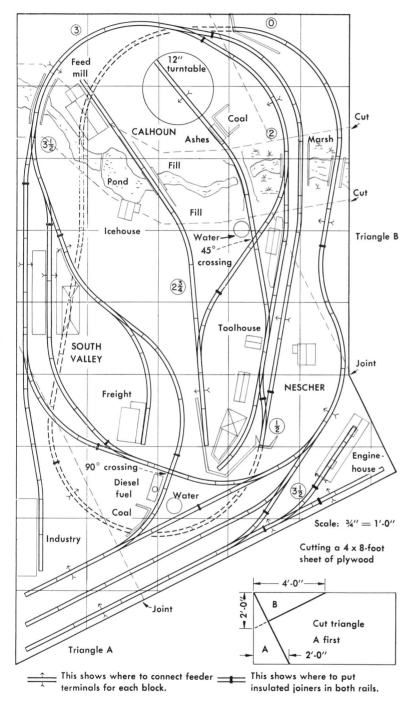

This shows where to connect feeder terminals for each block.   This shows where to put insulated joiners in both rails.

Fig. 18-3. The Nescher & South Valley Mineral RR. track plan with insulated rail joiners and feeder terminals indicated; compare with Fig. 18-2. This plan also shows how, by cutting the plywood as shown in the small detail drawing and then cutting the river depression, you can extend the 4 x 8-foot size to approximately 5'-6" x 9'-0" over all, with the narrow end 4'-8" wide. This makes the grade separation easier and greatly improves scenic possibilities between the tracks. Track elevations in inches are shown in circles on this drawing. Dotted trackage is in tunnel, hidden by scenery.

19: Adding control for loops and wyes

THE diagrams in chapter 17 were suitable for railroads of any size as long as there were no turning tracks, loops, wyes, turntables, return cutoffs, etc., in them. We learned what to do about these turning tracks without a control panel in chapter 9. Then in chapter 18 we learned that we may divide these turning tracks into blocks if they happen to be large enough to hold two trains at once. There is also the possibility that there is more than one place where there's a turning track.

Now our task is to provide whatever special wiring is needed for the blocks located in the turning tracks. The wiring would explain itself, if you could remember what we've discussed so far, but that's quite a lot to remember. What we will do is combine three control systems into one; see Fig. 19-1. Build one panel large enough to handle not only all the ordinary block wiring, as we did two chapters ago, but also two other sections. At the right we will now add block toggle switches for whatever number of blocks we happen to have in the return tracks. These are the

blocks we numbered and added the letter R (in the example, blocks 31R and 32R).

Finally, as shown at the bottom of Fig. 19-1, we'll add four more toggles for direction control (regardless of the size of the railroad). There will be a pair of these for each set of throttle controls. In each pair of these toggles, one will be marked "Main" and the other "Loop."

Notice now that jumper wire J no longer goes directly from one power pack to the other.

It must not.

The four toggles at the bottom of the diagram are each wired just like the direction controllers we discussed earlier in chapter 9 except that now we've done the scheme twice, once for each power pack.

The ordinary block toggles and feeders are wired the same as before, so for clarity we've shown them in lightweight lines in this diagram. However, note that they now get their power by way of the two "Main" direction control toggles; no longer are they powered direct from the throttle units on the packs.

Note carefully how the two new block toggles, one for each of the blocks that happen to be in the return track zone (and identified with the letter R), are wired. Of course, you might have more or fewer toggles here, depending on the number of blocks that happen to be in return-track zones. It will take you a little while to recognize the pattern of this new section of wiring for the return-track blocks, but it is easy to explain what this wiring does.

First, it allows you to determine which way you want a train to travel in the return-track zones. This is done individually for either throttle unit by means of the nearby "Loop" toggle.

Second, it allows you to connect any loop or return-track block to either power pack by flipping the appropriate block toggle at the upper right to the

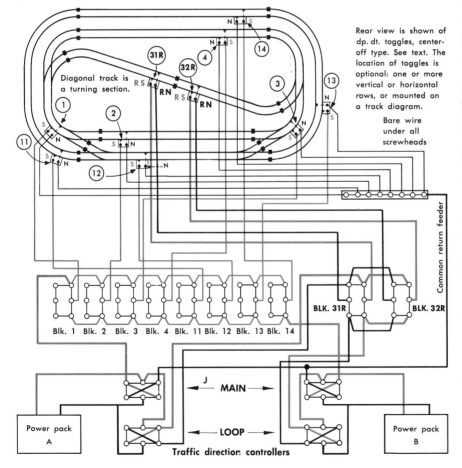

Rear view is shown of dp. dt. toggles, center-off type. See text. The location of toggles is optional: one or more vertical or horizontal rows, or mounted on a track diagram.

Bare wire under all screwheads

Fig. 19-1. Wiring for blocks in the turning track, using ordinary toggles.

left or right. Center is still "Off."

Will you allow me to repeat something, as it catches many a new modeler and some veterans off guard?

Back in chapter 17 we showed a jumper, J, connecting one power pack to the other. This was okay then, but taboo now. As soon as you have a return track on a railroad (wired with a common return feeder in this manner*) it is not permissible to have any wire running directly from any terminal of one power pack to any terminal of the other.

Don't say I didn't warn you. Notice that there still is a jumper J but that it now connects between the two mainline direction controller toggles, not the power packs.

Now let's do it with Atlas

I mentioned previously that while the Atlas Controller is intended for use in controlling return tracks, it is awkward to manipulate and it has the additional limitation of requiring one such controller device for each return-track block.

For about the same cost you can either use toggle switches for return-track control as we did in the previous diagram, or you can use Atlas Twin units. These will take less time to install.

Get two Twins for "Main" versus "Loop" direction control and mount these near their respective power packs as shown at the bottom of Fig. 19-2. Use them in the same way we used toggles for direction control, chapter 9. Then get an additional Atlas Twin for each block in return-track zones — the blocks to which you've added the letter R on the numbering plan. Mount these block Twins inverted as shown so the four connections are at the bottom.

If you want to control return-track block 31R from pack A, move the left slider up or down on the respective Twin unit 31R. The right-hand slider connects that same block to pack B. Be sure to move either slider to its center "Off" position before using the other or a short circuit between packs could develop. This is one of the disadvantages of this scheme.†

*As with all rules there is an exception to the warning, but that is only when the N rails are not fed through a common power return feeder but rather through added contacts on the block toggles in the manner we will use in the last control panel scheme of this book.

†I realize that at some time before the next printing of this book, the Atlas devices might be redesigned. In this case, perhaps controls for return-track blocks will be wired more in the manner of the toggle system of Fig. 19-1. If instruction sheets come with the Atlas products, the sheets will undoubtedly explain the application fully.

Ben Watkins of Lancaster, S. C., uses Atlas control units as well as some toggles to control his railroad. The round dial at left is a thermometer; it has nothing to do with the pike.

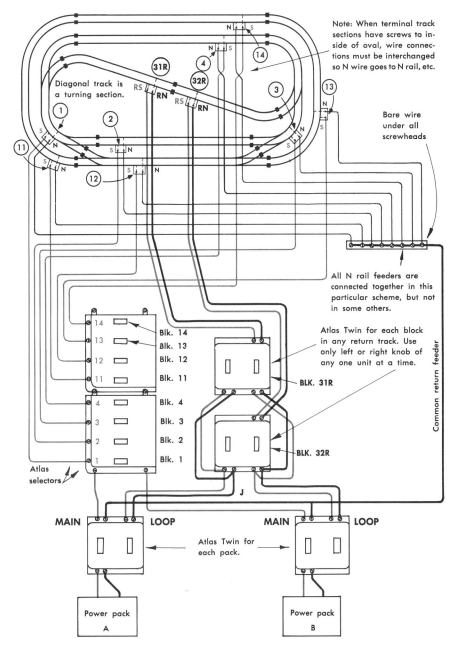

Fig. 19-2. Wiring for blocks in the turning track, using Atlas Twin units.

20: Building a control panel

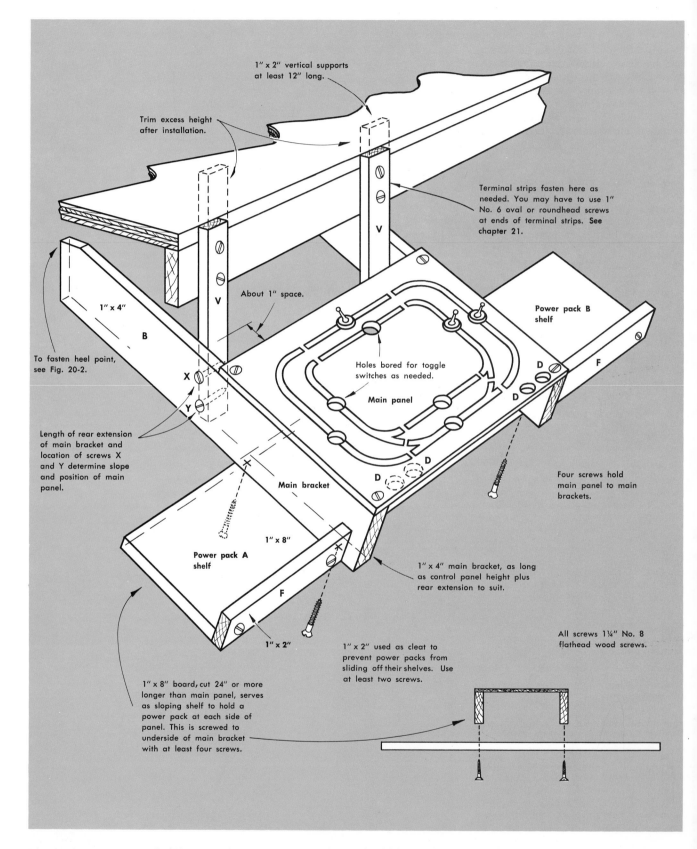

1" x 2" vertical supports at least 12" long.

Trim excess height after installation.

Terminal strips fasten here as needed. You may have to use 1" No. 6 oval or roundhead screws at ends of terminal strips. See chapter 21.

1" x 4"

B

About 1" space.

V

Power pack B shelf

To fasten heel point, see Fig. 20-2.

X

Y

Holes bored for toggle switches as needed.

Main panel

D

D

F

Length of rear extension of main bracket and location of screws X and Y determine slope and position of main panel.

Main bracket

D

D

Four screws hold main panel to main brackets.

Power pack A shelf

1" x 8"

1" x 4" main bracket, as long as control panel height plus rear extension to suit.

1" x 2"

F

1" x 2" used as cleat to prevent power packs from sliding off their shelves. Use at least two screws.

All screws 1¼" No. 8 flathead wood screws.

1" x 8" board, cut 24" or more longer than main panel, serves as sloping shelf to hold a power pack at each side of panel. This is screwed to underside of main bracket with at least four screws.

Fig. 20-1. An easy-to-build, convenient-to-use control panel which can be wired without working on the underside.

THERE are hundreds of good ways to build a control panel, and the one I'm describing in this chapter is a compromise between ease of construction and convenience in use. It is made of sizes of lumber you can get in every lumberyard and it requires only one size of wood screw throughout. It has one feature few other panel designs include — a shelf on each side for holding one or more power packs. It also has the feature that all wiring can be done without working on the underside of the panel. Thus, no hinges are needed. The terminal strips for connections will be directly in front of you and above panel level. If you feel the terminal strips are unsightly, you can devise a card or plywood cover for them.

First decide how large your panel itself must be. The space needed for each toggle switch measures roughly 1″ x 1½″ but this varies between makes. How many toggles you use for blocks and how you arrange them on the panel will determine the size of panel needed. You can make a cardboard mockup panel as a pattern.

As a rough rule for a map-type panel, you can allow about 2″ of panel length and width for each foot of length and width of your railroad table. To this add a little extra for margin space. Thus a panel for a 4 x 8 railroad table might well be made about 12″ x 18″. I wouldn't go much smaller than this formula unless you have a rather large railroad with rather long blocks, say about 8 feet each. You may want to add controls for remote turnouts on the panel and these will take more space.

When you arrange your panel front, leave space for four extra toggles, D in Fig. 20-1, at the lower corners of the panel. These can be side by side as shown, or one above the other. Don't drill all four holes, however, unless or until you have added a return track of some sort to your track plan (those blocks lettered R on the plan you made). One hole in each corner is adequate until then.

As suggested previously, the lines to represent track on a map-type panel can be simulated with cloth or paper masking tape, ¼″ or ⅛″ wide. Cut gaps in the tape to represent the boundaries between blocks and bore ½″ holes on the line at the most convenient point for the control toggle in each simulated block. Be sure to have the holes at least as far apart vertically and horizontally as the sizes of the toggles dictate. It isn't possible to put two toggles overlapping into the same space, but I've caught myself trying to do it more than once. Also, be sure not to get any toggles too near the edges of the panel where they would interfere with the supporting wood.

Materials

After you have decided on the size of the panel itself, you can determine the lengths of the other members of the control desk as you build. Follow the diagram in Fig. 20-1 as a guide. Materials needed are as follows:

● Main panel of ⅛″ or 3/16″ thick hardboard such as tempered Masonite.

● Two pieces of 1 x 4 lumber, 2½ to 3 times as long as the height of your panel front.

● At least 8 linear feet of 1 x 2 lumber, clear of knots, to make F and V, with some left over. If the lumberyard doesn't stock 1 x 2, you can saw a 1 x 4 down the middle, or use selected pieces of what is called "furring strip."

● One piece of 1 x 8 lumber, 2 feet longer than the length of your main panel. This is kept in one long piece and its ends serve as the sloping platforms for holding the power packs.

If your panel is more than 24″ long, you may also want to add lengthwise bracing of 1 x 2 lumber under the front and rear edges of the panel to keep it from sagging. This extra reinforcing is not shown in our diagram.

All lumber should be a good grade of clear white pine or sugar pine, or should be sawed from a sheet of ¾″ plywood.

For screws buy a gross of 1¼″ No. 8 flathead steel wood screws. About three dozen is all you need now, but this size will be very handy for other things around the railroad and gross lots save money if you buy them at a hardware store that sells to carpenters and other craftsmen.

To save yourself a lot of time, buy a Starrett 1¼″ No. 8 Screw Pilot. This is a special drill that makes a neat job of drilling two sizes of hole and a countersink cone all at once to receive the screws. It fits any ¼″ electric drill or can be used in a hand drill or brace.

Steps in assembly

Add pieces B, the side brackets, to your panel front. Next, fasten vertical brackets V to the side brackets

temporarily, using only one screw, X. Notice that these vertical brackets should be fastened about 1″ beyond the top edge of the panel. It is a good idea to make both the side brackets and the vertical pieces a little on the long side at first.

Now hold the vertical pieces against the side of the railroad table. Raise or lower them until the height at the rear of the panel is about where you want it. This will show how short you can cut pieces V, *but don't cut them yet*. Instead, fasten them to the railroad table side at the desired height with two screws each.

Now you can shorten the rear end of side brackets B until the amount of panel slope is what you want. It is usually good to have the front edge of the panel at least above your lap when sitting at the controls, and a little higher will make it easier to reach the toggles while you are standing.

The rear ends of the side brackets can be cut on a bias to seat better against the underside of the tabletop. It is a good idea to secure the rear ends to the table. A screw down from the top would work, but this is not good because you may find yourself covering it with scenery, structures, or track later on. In building any model railroad, it is best *never* to drive any screws down into or through the tabletop for this very reason. Always work from below so any screw can be removed at any time in the future. Part of the whole idea of model railroading is to keep making improvements, and a screw that you can't remove easily is a horrible handicap.

Hardware stores sell small bent L brackets that secure things to the underside of the tabletop with two screws. Use a block of wood between the bracket and the tabletop so the 1½″ screw doesn't run all the way out the top, or else use a shorter screw here. See Fig. 20-2.

After the rear ends of the side brackets are secured, add the second screws, Y, at the vertical supports. Finally, fasten the shelf for the power packs and the front lips, F.

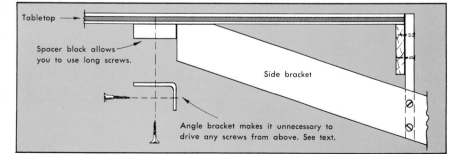

Fig. 20-2. **Easy method of attaching side brackets to underside of tabletop.**

21: The easiest wiring of all

EARLIER parts of this book went into some of the theory of control wiring, but the control panel we are about to wire doesn't require that you understand the theory. It will help if you do understand it, but even if you don't you can go ahead with this final control panel scheme merely by using a published track plan that's already divided into blocks.*

Actually, the wiring of this panel is the same as is used in the book *HO Railroad That Grows*. It looks a bit complicated but it isn't at all. Everything is simple repetition and you can hardly go wrong. If you do go wrong, the methods we use will allow you to correct an error quickly.

The control panel construction suggested in chapter 20 will be extremely convenient for this panel wiring.

First you do some counting

First, you count the blocks on the track plan you want to control. Blocks are sometimes numbered on published plans, but if they are not, they usually have some indication of where ter-

*Such plans can be found in the various track plan books published by Kalmbach Publishing Co. (especially *Track Plans for Sectional Track* and *101 Track Plans*).

minal connections to the S and N rails are to go. Arrowheads and arrowtails are commonly used, and the pair indicates the terminal connections for one block. Count all the pairs and you have the total number of blocks.

Notice whether the track plan has any turning track, loops, wyes, or return diagonal cutoffs, etc. We talked about how to locate these in chapter 9, and a more thorough discussion can be found in the book *How to Wire Your Model Railroad*. Also, on most published plans the letter R will be shown beside the block feeder symbols on turning-track blocks.

Parts needed

Now buy a dp. dt. co. (double-pole, double-throw, center-off) toggle switch for each and every block you counted. If you found one or more of the blocks in a turning-track zone, add four more of these same toggles. If not, add two more. Normally, the connecting terminals on toggles are made for soldered connections. However toggles are also made with screws for all six connections if you wish to avoid soldering.

You don't have to use the exact type of electric switch I've specified. Any kind of electric switch with at least two poles and at least three positions (leaving the middle position unconnected for "Off") could be substituted. However, most of our drawings will illustrate the common dp. dt. co. toggle, as it is the type most often sold in hobby shops.

Next, buy the same number of terminal strips, with at least six terminal connecting points per strip. Many hobby shops and all radio parts houses will have them. Again, you need at least six connecting places per strip. If there are more, that's all right as long as all the strips are the same. Note in the photo that I used a seven-terminal strip; the store was out of six-terminal strips at the time I made my purchase.

Terminal strips come in several varieties. The kind of strip to which you solder a wire at the rear and slip another wire under a screwhead at the front of each terminal will be by far the most convenient.

The terminal strips are going to be mounted in a horizontal row above the upper edge of the control panel. To do this you will have to add the two new strips of wood shown in Fig. 21-1. These should be so spaced that the screws for fastening each end of each terminal strip will go into the new wood strips. On the other hand, the wood should not interfere with the electrical connections at the back of the terminal strips.

The toggle-and-terminal units

The thing that is going to make wiring this control panel so easy is a sort of "prefab" assembly scheme we are about to follow. Each toggle is going to be connected to its associated terminal strip by six wires, Fig. 21-2. The route of each wire will follow an exact pattern that is duplicated for all other toggles. The length between toggle and its terminal strip will be the same for all units. This will waste a little wire because we don't always need this much length, but the advantages are complete interchangeability (in case of trouble) and less likelihood of making wiring mistakes.

Now, how much wire will we need? Look ahead and you'll see that the terminal strips are going to be mounted a little beyond the control

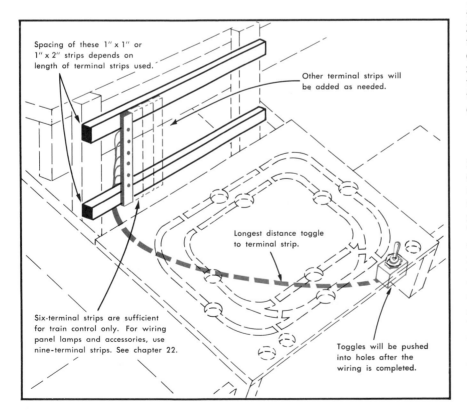

Spacing of these 1" x 1" or 1" x 2" strips depends on length of terminal strips used.

Other terminal strips will be added as needed.

Longest distance toggle to terminal strip.

Six-terminal strips are sufficient for train control only. For wiring panel lamps and accessories, use nine-terminal strips. See chapter 22.

Toggles will be pushed into holes after the wiring is completed.

Fig. 21-1. Wiring can be done very simply by this mass production scheme.

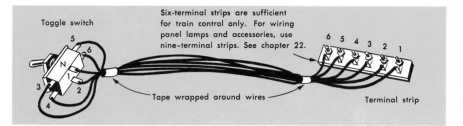

Fig. 21-2. Each control panel toggle can be wired exactly the same as the next and each will have its terminals available at the terminal strip attached to it by six wires. Cloth or paper masking tape holds wires neatly.

Final wiring steps

The two terminal strips at the farthest to the left can be lettered A and B. The controlled d.c. wires from power packs A and B (or from the two outputs of a two-throttle pack) should now be connected to terminals 1 and 2 at the top of these strips. Be sure they really are terminals 1 and 2 and not the other end, 5 and 6.

In Fig. 21-4 these power pack wires are shown in front of other items for clarity. Actually, you will sneak them behind as barely seen in Fig. 21-7 so they will be out of the way.

Going back to Fig. 21-4, push the toggle connected to terminal strip A into the lower left hole at the corner of the control panel.

You will find it easier to keep the toggles from loosening if you use the hexagon nut around the lever shank of the toggle switch on the upper side of the control panel and use the knurled ring (actually intended for the upper side) underneath the panel. This allows you to tighten the toggle in its place more securely with an open-end wrench. After a week or so, the toggles will need tightening again because the wood will yield a little.

Push the toggle associated with terminal strip B into the other "Main" hole near the lower right corner of the panel.

These toggles are the main direction controllers for throttles A and B and they determine which way is forward when you have the reverser on the power pack set normally for forward operation.

If you flip main toggle A to the right, the train should move in that direction when the power pack reverser at pack A is set for forward. If the train goes the wrong way, turn main toggle A 180 degrees around in its hole. Toggle B should be tested in the same way — but we're really ahead of ourselves now, for we don't have the track connected yet.

Now look at Fig. 21-5. Here the connections from each power pack are still shown in front for clarity, but of course you will sneak them be-

panel face. We want to be sure that the toggle that happens to be the farthest from its associated terminal strip will be provided with enough wire to reach the full distance. In general, a group of wires as long as the diagonal distance across the face of the control panel, plus about 6″ more, will usually do. The toggle most likely to need the longest cable of six wires is the one that goes from the hole at the lower right of the panel to the terminal strip located second from the extreme left, above the panel face. See Fig. 21-1. If the wires are long enough to make this span, all other toggle-terminal units will also fit. Multiply this length of wire by six times the number of toggles we bought and you have the total amount of wire needed. Add 10 per cent for safety.

The types of wire to use were suggested back on page 55 and information on soldering can be found on page 60. Be sure you do not use either non-corroding soldering paste or any kind of acid flux in the electrical work. If you do not want to do any soldering, I suggest you then buy solid rather than stranded wire in a small size (22 or 24) for these toggle-to-terminal connections. Then make the terminal end of each wire into a complete loop around the terminal screw so it will not come off when the screw is loosened later for other connections.

Add the wire in mass-production fashion

Note the way the terminals of the toggle switch are numbered in Fig. 21-3.* Start with the wire from toggle terminal No. 1 and connect it by a wire to the terminal strip terminal No. 1. Solder this wire at each end (or use loops if screw terminals are used).

Check this one-wire assembly to see if there is enough wire so the toggle can be pushed into the lower right hole and the terminal strip mounted at the upper left end of the terminal strip area. If the wire is long enough, go on to the next toggle and all the others, using the same length of wire each time to connect terminals No. 1 together.

After this, add wire No. 2 to every toggle and terminal. This should be just a little shorter since the terminal connecting point will be a step closer to the toggle.

After a little while you will have all the toggles and terminals joined into units, one unit for each block, plus the two or four extra toggle-terminal units mentioned before. Use two or more pieces of tacky electrical tape or paper masking tape (not household cellulose tape) to hold each group of six wires into a neat bundle, as in Fig. 21-2. Now mount the terminal strips for all track blocks so they bridge between the two wood strips of Fig. 21-1.

Put all the strips to serve ordinary track blocks at the left. Put the strips for toggles representing return tracks (if any) in another group at the right. These are the blocks marked R on published plans. Add two more strips to each group, and if you counted right you should come out even.

For the moment leave all the toggles themselves dangling below. At this stage the assembly will look something like that in Fig. 21-4, but the track design will, of course, be altered to correspond to your railroad.

*If the type of switch you chose was not of the same pattern as a dp. dt. toggle switch, the following will help you identify the terminals. Nos. 1 and 2 are to be the two moving poles of your switch. Nos. 3 and 4 are the terminals to which these poles connect when the switch is thrown to one side, the odd-numbered poles mating each other and the even-numbered mating each other. Connections 5 and 6 are the terminal contacts when the switch is thrown to its opposite extreme. If it is not apparent by examination how your switch is constructed internally, a hobby shop or radio repair employee can test your switch with an ohmmeter or continuity tester lamp and mark the terminals on a sample for you. Show him this paragraph as a guide.

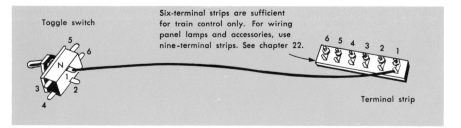

Fig. 21-3. Start the wiring with the first wire. Add it to all toggle-and-terminal units before going back to the first unit to add the second wire, and so on. The footnote, left, tells how to substitute other types of switches.

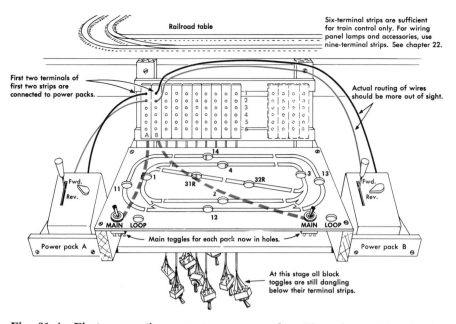

Six-terminal strips are sufficient for train control only. For wiring panel lamps and accessories, use nine-terminal strips. See chapter 22.

First two terminals of first two strips are connected to power packs.

Actual routing of wires should be more out of sight.

Main toggles for each pack now in holes.

At this stage all block toggles are still dangling below their terminal strips.

Power pack A

Power pack B

Fig. 21-4. First connections are to power packs. The wires will actually run behind instead of in front of the woodwork as shown here for clarity.

hind the woodwork when you install them. The really important things on Fig. 21-5 are the four horizontal "bus" wire connections that extend across most of the terminal strips at positions 3, 4, 5, and 6 vertically. These wires have a sort of J shape beginning with two terminal connections at the left and then connecting to one terminal point each for all the terminal strips that have a block number.

Note that the two colored wires that start at strip A make two connections each here, but skip past terminal strip B entirely. The other two wires start at two places each on strip B.

Except where protection might be

needed near terminal strip B where wires cross but must not touch, the four wires can have their insulation skinned off completely. This makes it easy to zigzag each wire under all the screw terminals to the right. Stranded wire can be used here but solid wire is less likely to cause trouble from the wandering of individual strands.

At the far end, these wires continue into space a short distance. This is so you can add more toggle-terminal units later if you wish to add more blocks to your railroad either by dividing some existing blocks in two or after laying more track.

After the J-shaped bus wires are in

place, you are ready to connect the wires that come from the various blocks of the track.

The wires from N rails (inner rail of the various ovals) go to terminal 1 on their respective terminal strips. The S wires go to terminal 2.

Connect just one block first and then make a test. We show block 14 connected in Fig. 21-5. You should now be able to run a train back and forth in block 14 from either power pack and in either direction by merely manipulating toggle 14 (shown now installed in its hole), the two main toggles, and the power pack throttle levers and reversing switches. If this block doesn't seem to work, disconnect the track wires and find another block that does work. After you have one block working correctly, finding trouble in other blocks will be easier.

Turn toggle 14 in its hole so it points toward whichever power pack is operating its block when flipped in that direction.

Before connecting any more track wires, run the train slowly back and forth while you flip all the other dangling toggles to the left, then the right and back to center, one at a time. If any of the other toggles affect the train in block 14, that toggle is miswired to its terminal strip.

Next, connect an adjoining block to its terminal strip. The train should now be able to move freely from one block to the next. If it goes the wrong direction in the new block, you probably have the S and N wires from the track to terminals 1 and 2 of the new strip connected the wrong way around. Interchange them.

Very likely, you will find all the wiring is all right, and soon you will have connected the last track block and pushed the last toggle into the appropriate hole of the control panel. Do all the wiring for the main group of blocks before going on to any blocks that are in the return track areas (blocks marked with an R).

If you have trouble

If there is trouble, you can tell if it is in the track or toggle by moving the track wires to another toggle terminal unit that you know is wired correctly.

Trouble in the track can be an open circuit or a short circuit. If it is an open circuit, it will affect a train only in the defective area, but a short circuit affects trains everywhere when the block toggle is turned on for the defective block.

Open circuits are caused by bad connections in the wiring, the toggle itself, loose rail joiners, or even by dirt on the rails.

Short circuits come from wires

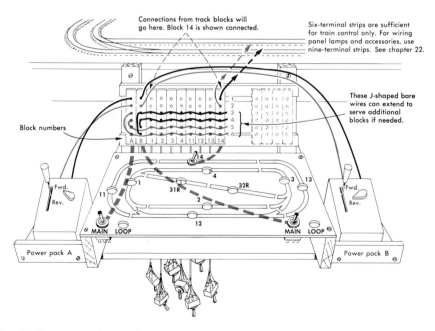

Connections from track blocks will go here. Block 14 is shown connected.

Six-terminal strips are sufficient for train control only. For wiring panel lamps and accessories, use nine-terminal strips. See chapter 22.

These J-shaped bare wires can extend to serve additional blocks if needed.

Block numbers

Power pack A

Power pack B

Fig. 21-5. Mass of terminal strips is sometimes called a "matrix." Next step is to add horizontal "bus" connections. See text for important details.

touching each other where they shouldn't, from rails touching each other in switches and crossings where they shouldn't, from missing or defective rail gaps or insulated joiners, and even from rails, wires, or spikes touching metallic objects or scenery screen at two places where they shouldn't.

Short circuits can also happen in the wheels or other electrically insulated parts of the cars or engine.

The way to locate the exact place of a short is by gradual elimination of part of the wiring until the trouble is localized.

To locate an open circuit you work from the power pack out toward the track and then toward the train with a lamp or some other indicator that shows how far the plus and minus electric continuity is reaching. This kind of troubleshooting is thoroughly treated in the book *How to Wire Your Model Railroad*.

Don't forget to plug in the power pack! And turn it on!

Now for return loops, etc.

The terminal strips for the block or blocks you might have in return-track territory as explained in chapters 9 and 18 (blocks numbered with letter R attached) should now be placed in the terminal matrix area. (Sometimes this kind of wiring is called a "matrix" system.) Also, put

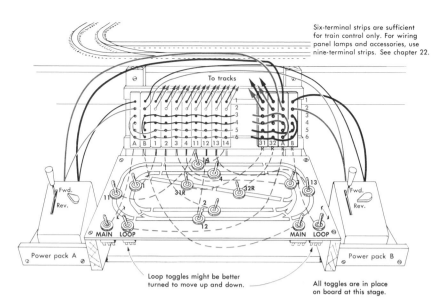

Fig. 21-6. If you have return loops, wyes, a turntable track, or return cut-off in your track pattern, add another matrix; wire in repetitive fashion.

the two strips, AR and BR, at the far right. These last have their terminals 1 and 2 connected directly to the power pack output terminals just as was done earlier with strips A and B. All the wiring goes on as before with four new J bus wires. Put the toggles in their proper holes in the control panel face. See Fig. 21-6.

This matrix scheme makes wiring in this particular way easy. It also allows you to easily adapt your wiring

to a wider variety of all kinds of power packs, and it doesn't matter whether your track wiring is for the "common return rail" type mentioned earlier or not. You can use this panel in many ways. Some were described in earlier chapters of this book.

Fig. 21-7 shows a finished matrix wiring scheme that was the last step of a similar control panel described, along with many other useful ideas, in the book *HO Railroad That Grows*.

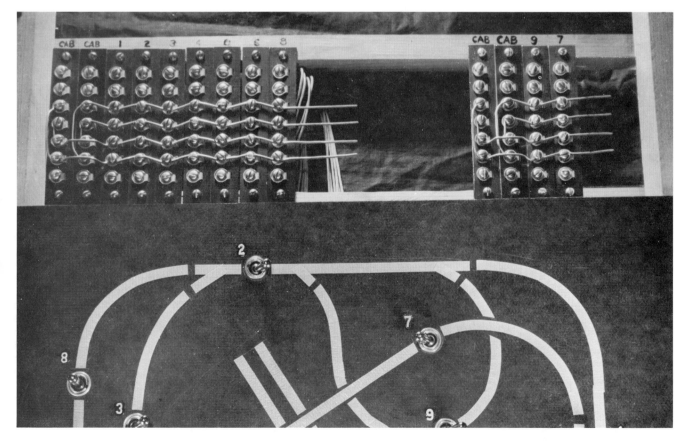

Fig. 21-7. This slightly different control panel was built for "HO Railroad That Grows," described in another book.

A nicely weathered Santa Fe Consolidation streaks by on its way to San Rafael as old No. 6 emerges from Corte Madera Tunnel on the Shedd Short Line RR. The pike belongs to Robert Shedd; the two locomotives are the property of Chuck Barnard.

Along the right of way

Giant sequoia trees on the logging railroad of Alan Armitage dwarf the Climax locomotive and its string of log bogies. Note how carefully the painted backdrop was made to blend with the foreground scenery; the scene is actually only about 3 feet deep. Below is another view emphasizing the spectacular scenery on the railroad. Tomahawk station was built from styrene plastic sheet.

This pleasant little scene was photographed on the Marshall Feehan railroad in Spokane, Wash. The railroad features old-time rolling stock and small steam-type locomotives. This is what is called a period pike — that is, all or almost all of the equipment fits into a particular era. A modern period pike might be one with all-diesel power and new large-capacity cars.

22: Easy wiring for lamps and accessories

THE matrix method of wiring we just used for block control wiring can be extended to simplify the wiring of anything around the railroad where a number of things are controlled in the same manner.

One of the most useful additions you can make to a control panel is to have lamps light up in the various blocks when in use. This is easy to do if you use some kind of block control switch that has an extra pole. A number of so-called "wafer" or "rotary" switches are available in 3p. 3t. form or 4p. 3t. form. The first two poles of such a switch are wired just as described in the preceding chapter. Then an extra pole is used for controlling the panel lamp so it goes on when *either* cab (power pack A or B) is using the block.

If you follow the details of Fig. 22-1 you'll get the idea. The particular switch used is a Mallory 3243J, and the terminal connections are labeled in our drawing. Most other makes and kinds of switch are built more openly so you can see how the contacts work and thus identify which is which. For this scheme you would use terminal strips of at least 9 connecting places each. Terminals 1 through 6 are wired to the track as before, complete with J-shaped bus wires, etc.

Terminals 7 and 8 are to be connected to your lighting power source — any voltage suitable to the panel lamps you use. If you should wish to have more than one lamp light up when a block is in use, additional

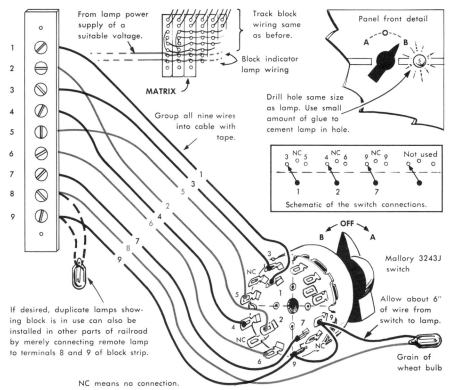

Fig. 22-1. How to wire a Mallory 3243J switch to indicate block occupancy.

lamps can be connected between terminals 8 and 9 and located anywhere.

To connect the lighting power to all lamps, add bus wires across all terminals 7 from left to right and also across all terminals 8 in the same way. Then connect one end of these two bus wires to the transformer or other power source you have selected

for lamps. This is discussed in chapter 15.

The lamps you add to toggles A, B, AR, and BR (Fig. 21-6) are optional. They will go off when you throw the switch to disconnect the power pack from all track. This can be a handy feature.

After installing this matrix scheme for blocks, you might consider its advantages for remote control of switch machines and any other accessory features. In all cases, horizontal bus wires can be used to supply the running power to any number of toggles to control accessories.

In Fig. 22-2 the wiring for lamps and other accessories controlled by on-off (sp. st.) toggles is shown as one example of this application. For this, terminal strips of only three terminals each are needed.

One of the big advantages of this matrix system is that no matter how you change the track, or even if you build another railroad, the wiring can be saved. All you do is make a new panel front with holes in new locations and push the already-wired toggles into the new hole locations.

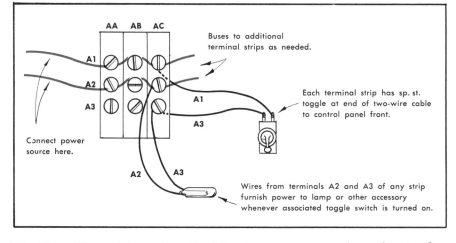

Fig. 22-2. The matrix system of wiring lamps or accessories, using toggles.

23: Tools for model railroading

VERY few tools are needed for most of the kits in HO but you might as well plan right now to eventually spend at least $10 and perhaps more on tools. You may have some of the needed tools left over from other hobbies; if so, all the better. Be sure you don't try to get along with misfit tools, however. For instance, a sharp screwdriver of the right blade width to match its screw should always be used. Wrong-size drivers or those with rounded edges are likely to get you into difficulties, such as breaking or mangling screws, or marring the surface of a model near the screw.

In this chapter I'll list the 10 or so tools I think you need most, then comment on others I've found helpful.

Mill file

A smooth single-cut mill file about 6" long is very handy for removing flash from die-cast metal and molded plastic parts. It's also useful for making any surface smooth and flat. A file cuts by rolling minute shavings from the surface of the work. Always lift it on the back stroke so you don't wear flat tops on the file teeth. If the file makes a low buzzing noise and cuts a waffle pattern in the work, clamp the work more securely and file from another direction.

Buy a low-cost handle for your file; it may save you from a painful accident.

Files are sold in hardware stores. Better grades are wrapped in paper so one file won't dull the next.

Watercolor brush

Watercolor brushes have about the right qualities for model work. A good brush can lay paint on your models almost as evenly as a sprayer, and it will keep a single point so you can use it for both broad strokes and fine lettering. Size 3 holds about the right amount of paint for model work. For painting large structures, get a much larger brush.

Clean the brush thoroughly so no paint dries near the base of the hairs. Otherwise the hairs will break off later and spoil some of your work. Use the same thinner recommended for the paint you've just used.

Modeler's knife

It's hard to say whether files or a modeler's knife get the most use in kit building. The knife can take a lot of punishment because the blades are replaceable. You can use the knife on thin metal flash as well as for all kinds of wood, plastic, and cardboard cutting.

Knives are also handy for picking up small coil springs — you wedge the point into the coils near the end of the spring and then lift the spring into the coupler or truck frame.

Fig. 23-1 shows X-acto knife No. 1, which comes with a pointed blade. I prefer blade style 16, shown above the knife. Don't press too hard with the modeler's knife; it cuts almost as fast with light pressure. The light cut will be more accurate than a heavy one.

Pin vise

The pin vise is actually a collet with a handle, something like a drill chuck. Most often you use it to hold small drills while drilling holes for ladders, screws, etc. It will also hold small taps while threading holes, and you can use it to hold small parts while painting or cleaning flash.

You'll need pin vises of several sizes. The vise shown in the drawing contains two double-ended collets, giving a total of four sizes all in one tool. The handle head can be removed when you chuck long rods or wire, which can then pass all the way through. While it costs more, you may prefer to get a set of separate pin vises, one in each of three or four sizes.

Drills

The four sizes of twist drills shown will do about 90 per cent of your model work. Five other sizes are fairly commonly used, making the whole list look like this: Nos. 42, 50, 52, 56, 60, 65, 70, 75 and 76. These will take care of almost every pin, nail, escutcheon, wire, grabiron, ladder, screw, and screw thread used in model kit assembly. If your instructions call for use of a $1/16''$ drill, you can use No. 52. It is only .001" larger.

High-speed drills will last longer than carbon drills if you plan to operate them with any kind of motor device. Carbon drills will do for hand operation only; they cost a little less.

When drilling, you'll find the drills won't break as easily as you might expect, but a sideways bend, or clogging of material in the drill flute, can jam the drill and break it. This jamming occurs most often in soft metals like lead, type metal, and other soft alloys such as are found in Walthers, Red Ball, and Selley kits. Remove the drill frequently to clear the chips and use a small amount of oil (beeswax is better) while drilling with small drills.

If drilling with a motor in plastic, avoid high speeds, as the drill point may melt the plastic and make a very large irregular hole. Drilling by hand is usually fast enough for wood and plastic as well as thin metals.

For drilling locations accurately, prick a small dot in the metal (at the point where you want to drill) with a prick punch and then enlarge the dot with a center punch. These simple tools are sold in hardware stores and some hobby shops.

Needle files

These are also called jeweler's files and they come in many different shapes and lengths. Advanced workers buy them in sets. Probably the two most useful shapes are flat and round in lengths of around 5".

Use the files for cleaning flash and removing material for a better fit between metal parts, and sometimes wood and plastic parts. Use the same care as for the mill file.

Screwdrivers

Screwdrivers are so familiar that we take them for granted. But small screwdrivers often have to do a much bigger job for their size than large ones, so it pays to take better-than-average care of them. Don't use a screwdriver as a prying tool or as a cutting tool unless you know how to grind a new sharp point on it without getting the point too hot. Keep the screwdriver sharp so it won't slip off a screw. Always select a screwdriver with a blade as wide as the screwhead. This is usually a size bigger than you think at first glance.

In model work you need a screwdriver with a blade $1/8''$ wide for truck-mounting screws, and smaller blades for other screws. The Moody screwdriver shown has interchangeable blades providing three commonly needed smaller sizes.

Side cutters

Pliers are more expensive than any of the other tools shown here and it pays to get a good quality of tool. These side cutters are used for clipping the ends of wire, small nails and screws, and even the ends of small shapes of stripwood for a rough cut before dressing with a file. They will be damaged if you use them on music wire or other springy steel. The side cutter or "nipper" shown is a small 4½" size made by Kraeuter & Co., one of the best-known makers of pliers.

Chain-nose pliers

These are also called needle-nose pliers. They are the most useful of the many kinds of pliers you might add to your tool kit. Later on you'll want a pair with a round nose for bending shapes in wire, and perhaps still later you'll want a pair of square-nose pliers.

Do not use these small pliers for tightening nuts or any operation that twists the jaws sideways. I keep a small pair of "dime-store" quality pliers around for such jobs that might be rough on the tool.

Additional tools

Very soon you'll have about all the tools you'll absolutely need, and then any others would be just for convenience. I think tweezers come next, and you should grind their points so they pick up the smallest parts easily. A model hammer is also essential, as well as some small anvil or flat object to hammer against. Sometimes a small magnifying glass on a stand is a help.

Next come taps for threading holes for screws. Size 2-56 does most of the work, followed by 0-80 and 00-90. Size 1-72 is not used as often. Sets come with the four sizes and a holder; or you can buy the 2-56 or others separately. The following table shows the proper drill to use (a very near size will often do) for making the hole before tapping it. The last column shows the hole that will let the screw pass through freely.

TAP	TAP DRILL	CLEAR DRILL
2-56	50	42
1-72	53	47
0-80	55	51
00-90	63	55

Turn the tap inward about a half turn, then back a quarter turn, doing this alternately so chips will break off and fall out of the hole.

Metric-size screws are used in most imported models and there are taps made in metric sizes should you need them.

Other most useful tools are the razor saw and miter block for it, scale rule, diemaker's square, set of small socket wrenches, small vise, oilstone, small soldering iron, scissors, scriber, and if you can afford it, a motor tool with abrasive cutoff wheels, abrasive cloth and paper disks, high-speed steel cylindrical-shape cutting burrs, and preferably a built-in chuck to take any size drill.

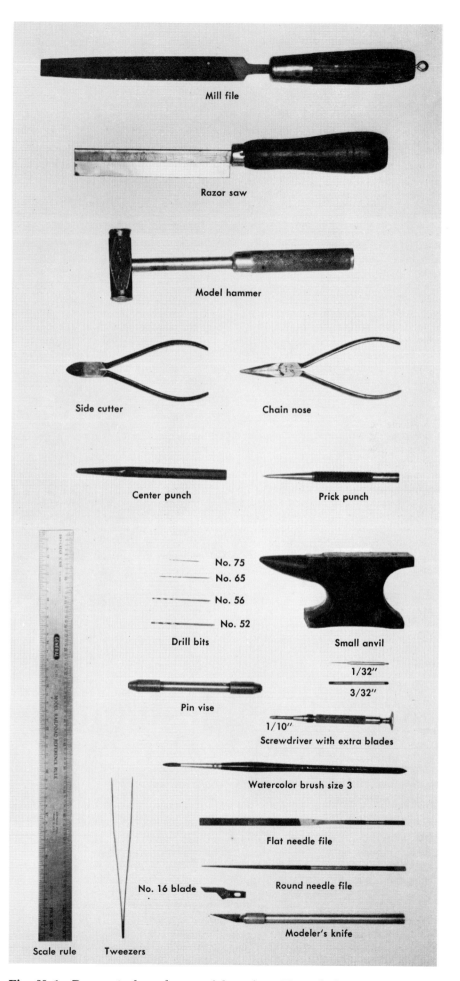

Fig. 23-1. **Proper tools make any job easier. Most of these are essential.**

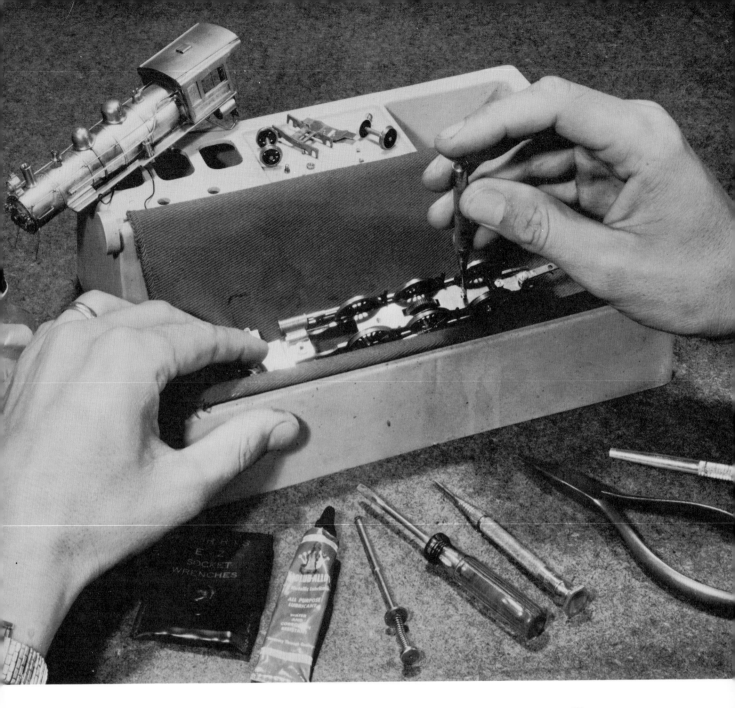

Troubleshooting guide

Index